# BUSES

## YEARBOOK 2019

Edited by STEWART J. BROWN

KEY PUBLISHING

# BUSES
## YEARBOOK 2019

FRONT COVER: *Nottingham City Transport has invested heavily in new buses from Alexander Dennis.* John Robinson

BACK COVER (UPPER): *The striking livery of the Halifax Joint Committee on former London Transport Routemaster RM1214.* Tony Wilson

BACK COVER (LOWER): *Zoo branding on a Lothian Buses Volvo.* Richard Walter

PREVIOUS PAGE: *An ADL Enviro400 of Lloyd's of Machynlleth passes through Furnace in 2013.* John Young

Published by Key Publishing Ltd.
www.keypublishing.com

First Published July 2018

**ISBN:** 978-1-912205-72-1

Printed in England by
Gomer Press Ltd
Llandysul Enterprise Park
Llandysul
Ceredigion
SA44 4JL

**www.busesmag.com**

# Delaine Buses

ABOVE: *Newest double-deckers in the Delaine fleet are three Wright Gemini 3-bodied Volvo B5TLs with the bodybuilder's 'classic' front. This is the second of them, 162, leaving Glinton on the trunk service 101 to Peterborough.* Stephen Whiteley

Buses editor **ALAN MILLAR** tells the story of one of Britain's few surviving family-owned local bus service operators from the pre-deregulation era, still thriving in south Lincolnshire and Peterborough as it reaches the 100th anniversary of its first motorbus

D elaine Buses — The Delaine if you prefer — is a rare example of the type of operator that is the stuff of enthusiasts' dreams.

This family-owned independent ticks all of the boxes of what makes a bus company special. It runs a frequent service on what before October 1986 were called stage carriage routes, mainly with double-deckers. Most of the fleet has been owned since new and is replaced on a planned basis. All its buses are painted and maintained in a smart, traditional two-tone blue and cream livery that succeeds in not looking outmoded. Every bus has a fleet number in a logical sequence. And the routes also have numbers.

The founding family — now into its fifth and sixth generations — still owns the business, works in it every day and has presided over not just its survival but its controlled growth in a small corner of England largely untouched by major operators. Unlike a great many independent operators down the years, there is no game plan to cash in on the investment and sell the company to a larger operator. The family is in it for the long-term.

This was one of few independent stage carriage operators still running in 1986 and over 30 years on is an even rarer survivor, which reaches a

ABOVE: *Members of the Delaine-Smith family in 2015. Left to right are Ian, Mark, Jennifer, Anthony and Kevin.* Steven Knight

major milestone in 2019 with the centenary of the introduction of its first motorbus — a 14-seat Ford Model T.

The company, based for all its existence in the south Lincolnshire market town of Bourne, is even older than that. It was already established as a general contractor in 1890 when founder's son William Smith began carrying passengers on its horse-drawn vehicles. It ran motor taxis from 1910 and introduced its first motorbus in 1919 to provide market day services linking Bourne with Spalding,

Stamford and Grantham, and started a trunk service south to Peterborough — the cornerstone of its 21st century operation — in 1923.

When William Smith died in 1913, his son Thomas Arthur took over and two years later married Emma Jane Weston from whose family the name Delaine emanated. The name Delaine was bestowed upon their son Hugh as a second name and he then bestowed it upon his children until the family name was eventually changed to Delaine-Smith in 1961. In an age when pioneering bus companies often identified

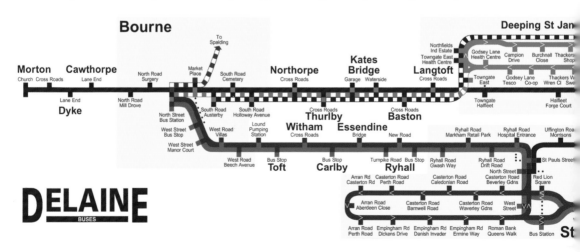

themselves with the sort of name found on sailing craft or hostelries, this one became The Delaine.

Thomas Arthur Smith lived until 1958, succeeded then by his son Hugh, who remained chairman and managing director until he died in 1995, shortly after being appointed MBE for his services to public transport in the New Year Honours List. His four sons were already in the business and today eldest son Ian is chairman, Anthony is managing director, while Kevin and youngest son Mark are directors. Anthony's daughters Jennifer and Victoria have held roles in the company since leaving school in 2010 and 2016 respectively.

Up to five members of the family drive at peak times on schooldays, reflecting the hands on nature of the business.

Hugh's sister Beryl worked continually in the business for 71 years before she retired owing to ill health in 2010 and died two years later. Her late husband Derek Tilley achieved 53 years' service with the company.

The family moved on to the current site in 1900 from the next street, Eastgate, and the depot has expanded over the years. It incorporates the sites of Bourne's two legendary motor racing teams' works, that of English Racing Automobiles (ERA) acquired in 1939 and British Racing Motors (BRM) in 1984. A 1972 property acquisition saw the rear of the premises reach Eastgate.

## Route network

The fleet has grown to 29 vehicles, but — family included — only has a staff of 34, 31 of whom hold PCV licences. Typical large operators will have at least two employees for every bus. This is a ship that is run tight.

At the core of the operation are three interurban routes on corridors linking Bourne with Peterborough. Both of these communities have grown in recent decades. Peterborough, a cathedral city and industrial town on the borders of the East Midlands and East Anglia, was designated a new town in 1967 principally to house part of the overspill population from London. Bourne has grown as a commuter town for Peterborough, its population almost tripling over the past 50 years to around 15,000.

The routes only acquired numbers as recently as 1992. The 101 runs half-hourly between Peterborough and Bourne, with an hourly extension northwards to the village of Morton. The hourly 102 adds a third journey between Peterborough and The Deepings — Market Deeping and Deeping St James — with all journeys extending to Bourne at peak times. Off-peak, buses leave Peterborough for The Deepings on the hour, quarter past and half past.

The third of these is the hourly 201/202, linking Peterborough and Bourne via Stamford, the main service passing Key Publishing's premises on the Ryhall Road on the Bourne side of Stamford. Until January 2016, these were separate routes. The then two-hourly 202 linked Bourne and Stamford, communities served by Delaine motorbuses since the original Model T arrived in 1919. The hourly 201 linked Stamford and Peterborough, replacing Barton Transport's route 101 when it pulled out of Stamford in 1988, and had been doubled in frequency from an initially two-hourly operation.

Merging them into one created new cross-town connections in Stamford, which like Peterborough — but not Bourne since 1959 — has a railway

BELOW: *The 2018 Delaine route network displayed in the style of a London Underground map.*

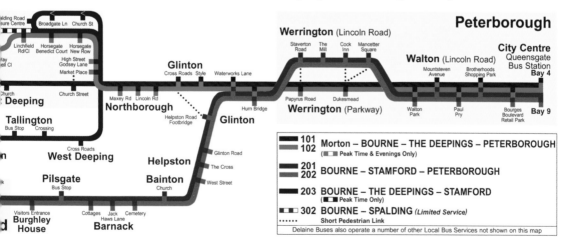

ABOVE: *The third of the Wright Gemini 3-bodied Volvo B5TLs, 163, northbound through the village of Newborough on a 101 journey from Peterborough to Bourne and Morton.* Alan Millar

station. The main benefit is that it now links housing estates on the west of the town with a hospital and retail parks on the east side, effectively adding a town service to the two routes already in existence. Ridership has grown as a result.

London Underground-style schematic maps — developed since first introduced in 1988 and produced in collaboration with a print company in Stamford — convey the extent of the network in a way that occasional as well as regular passengers should find easy to understand.

A crucial change made from the mid 1980s was to recognise that in an area with high car ownership, Delaine

must offer competitive journey times. That is easier to achieve in Peterborough where the new town is built around dual carriageways — known as parkways — that bypass the longer established local roads.

Delaine buses used to reach the city centre along one of the old highways, the Lincoln Road that follows the old alignment of the A15. But, starting with the hourly Deeping St James to Peterborough service in 1985 which became known affectionately by locals as The Deepings Flyer, a model eventually adopted by all Delaine services within the city with peak Bourne journeys in 1990 and all journeys from 1992, it took the more direct route along the Werrington Parkway and its continuation, Bourges Boulevard, to offer the quickest route in and out of town.

It may miss out the intermediate communities within Peterborough, but Anthony Delaine-Smith says it more

*The newest of the five East Lancs Vyking-bodied Volvo B7TLs, 140, operating a college day only late afternoon 301 working from Bourne in October 2017. It has just departed the village of Billingborough, and is on its way along the country lanes to Folkingham and Aslackby.* Stephen Whiteley

than makes up for this by providing longer distance passengers with a more attractive service. Slow progress along the old route, he says, deterred out-of-town passengers from considering the bus.

The Stamford service deviates to serve the shopping centre in the enlarged village of Werrington, on the edge of Peterborough, but still reaches the city centre in less than half the time taken by more frequent Stagecoach local routes.

Ironically both parkways soon required bus stop lay-bys to be installed close to each pedestrian underpass to accommodate the growing number of passengers who preferred to use the quicker service into the city centre.

Journey times on the 101/102 also benefit from the way that the Lincolnshire villages between Peterborough and Bourne have been built. These are largely east-west linear developments along the north-south A15, so there is no need for buses to divert off the main road to reach shops or many of the homes. Indeed, usually just one bus stop suffices for each settlement, helping the buses make brisk progress with fewer stops. The company specifies its buses with high-speed back axles for interurban running.

## Schools and colleges

While these routes form the bedrock of the business and have experienced growth, the requirement for as many as 29 buses — all but seven of them double-deck — stems from the expansion of commercial services since deregulation to cater for commuters into Peterborough and those making rail connections to London. Another significant growth factor is catering for students at eight schools and colleges sited on

BELOW: *Wright Eclipse Urban-bodied Volvo B7RLE 146, previously with Perryman's of Berwick, on the Thursdays-only market day 09.07 departure of route 301 from Aslackby to Bourne via the villages. It was pictured on Billingborough Road, between Folkingham and Billingborough. The return journey from Bourne is at 12.10.* Stephen Whiteley

ABOVE: *The East Lancs Olympus-bodied Volvo B9TLs are named after past members of the family. This is 142, named Thomas Arthur Smith, passing through Glinton on route 101.* Stephen Whiteley

ABOVE: *Wright Eclipse Gemini 2-bodied Volvo B9TL 156 in Thackers Way, Deeping St James on the hourly 102 service between Peterborough and the Deepings.* Stephen Whiteley

ABOVE: *Although dedicated to schools services, the two ex-Dublin Bus Volvo B7TLs with Alexander ALX400 bodies are painted in full fleet livery and have Select registrations similar to those on the double-deckers purchased new. This is 160 on the afternoon 302 journey from Bourne to Spalding.* Stephen Whiteley

or close by core Delaine routes, all of which run as registered routes available to the general public.

In many parts of the country, there are routes that do not start until after the schools are in and also have mid-afternoon gaps in their schedules while

ABOVE: *The bespoke Delaine seat moquette in one of the Wright Gemini 3-bodied Volvo B5TLs.* Alan Millar

their buses go off to carry children home again. Delaine school journeys operate differently, being overlaid upon the core schedule for the interurban routes. Some cover sections of the main routes as duplicate journeys, while others strike out to places beyond them. For all of them, the students — or their parents — pay for their travel, primarily with season tickets, as do the local authorities for students entitled to free home to school transport, who benefit from only

BELOW: *Willowbrook-bodied Leyland Titan PD2/20 45 in Bourne during a Delaine running day in 2015.* Nick Thomson

buying the number of tickets they require on a service rather than having to hire a vehicle.

Their growth has come in large part from the introduction of parental choice, allowing pupils to attend state schools deemed to best meet their needs, regardless of where they live. So Bourne Grammar School, where mid-afternoon the forecourt turns briefly into a busy mini bus station, attracts pupils from as far away as Peterborough, Spalding and Stamford.

The clever part of this is that many of the student movements run against the flow of adult commuter travel, so early morning journeys carry early bird and London-bound commuters from Bourne into Peterborough, then return with students heading for the grammar school. The flow of traffic is reversed in the afternoons. By working closely with schools and colleges, Delaine has been able to tailor those services to meet the establishments' requirements.

These commercial developments help explain why this company has not just survived while so many independents have disappeared, but has prospered. It also owes its survival to what it does not do. Unlike many others, it runs no tendered services for local authorities, just commercial services, so is not exposed to the volatility of that market within the economic cycle and when routes change hands on

*The Yeates-bodied Leyland Titan PD3/1, 50, taking part in the same 2015 running day. It is on the A15, heading towards Northorpe with the final heritage working of the day, the 17.20 departure from Peterborough to Bourne. More recent running days are held over the Bourne-Stamford route.*
Stephen Whiteley

re-tendering and competition drives down the rate for the job.

'Always work with the local authority, not for them' was a mantra followed by Hugh Delaine-Smith when he ran the company and is one of many of his rules in life that his sons have continued to follow.

Similarly, although many of its passengers take advantage of the free concessionary travel scheme for older people — within Lincolnshire this operates 24hr a day, seven days a week — the majority of the clientele is younger and pays fares. It is less dependent on local authority reimbursement for free travel than operators who rely upon it for the bulk of their revenue.

The 101 runs on Sundays — in common with a few trunk and urban services across Lincolnshire — with the first weekday departure out of Bourne at 06.20 in time for long-distance commuters to catch a train from Peterborough into London. The last evening journey departs Peterborough at 20.15 and reaches Bourne at 20.55, which is a typical finishing time for a trunk route in the county. Although there is little demand for a service any later than that, as there is little nightlife in Peterborough, another of Hugh Delaine-Smith's mantras still followed is that to retain good staff avoid unsocial hours.

Delaine also benefits from how area agreements structured the bus industry 90 years ago to create dominant groups. Before all the upheaval of 1986,

Peterborough was on the edge of big operators' territories. Eastern Counties was the dominant local player, with United Counties coming in from the west as far as Stamford. Lincolnshire Road Car lay to the north, but had little presence south of Grantham.

Delaine reached an early accommodation with Peterborough Electric Traction (later absorbed into Eastern Counties) soon after the introduction of the 1930 Road Traffic Act and was able to develop this corner of England largely as its own.

## From Leyland to Volvo

All 22 double-deckers and seven single-deckers are Volvos with UK-built bodywork. Twenty of the double-deckers were bought new and the company aims to keep the fleet up to date by purchasing three new vehicles every two years, all funded from profits.

It moved to Volvo after buying mainly Leylands from 1930, supplemented in past decades by Bedfords when it ran coaches, and has operated double-deckers since purchasing a Willowbrook-bodied Crossley in 1948. It appreciates the level of aftersales backup that Volvo can provide, as an international bus and truck manufacturer and specifically from its local family-run truck and bus centre in Pinchbeck, which is only nine miles from Bourne.

Delaine has bought new vehicles from the start of motorbus operation and generally purchases secondhand only as a stopgap measure or in order

ABOVE: *Privately-preserved Leyland Atlantean 60, a Willowbrook-bodied PDR1/2, at the 2017 Buses Festival at the British Motor Museum.* Alan Millar

to change something quickly, as it did at the turn of the 1980s and 1990s when ten Duple Dominant-bodied Leyland Tigers, new to London Country as Green Line dual-purpose coaches, accelerated the replacement of its last Bedfords. It bought ex-Greater Manchester Leyland Atlanteans when seatbelt legislation prompted its decision to pull out of the coach business and fully concentrate on running buses, which had always been the primary activity.

The occasional availability of low mileage used vehicles has also provided an opportunity to buy secondhand examples of types already in the fleet. For example, it bought a pair of Northern Counties-bodied Leyland Atlantean AN68s in the 1970s when Maidstone Borough Council decided to get rid of all its double-deckers and followed this in 1980 with an AN68 — its first-ever bus with an Alexander body — new to Cunningham of Paisley, which had sold out to Western SMT, which kept none of the acquired fleet.

Aside from the new B8RLE, today's single-deckers — six Volvo B7RLEs with Wright Eclipse Urban bodies — came from other independent fleets that replaced their vehicles at around five years old.

Five of them have Euro3 engines, one coming from Perryman's of Berwick-upon-Tweed in 2009, the others from Whitelaw's of Stonehouse in Lanarkshire in 2009-11. The newest, with Euro4 engine, is a 2008 model from the Jim Stones fleet in Greater Manchester, which Delaine bought in 2013 and regards as possibly the best pre-owned single-decker it has ever owned.

The only secondhand double-deckers are a pair of Alexander ALX400-bodied Volvo B7TLs new to Dublin Bus in 2001 and acquired solely for schools journeys when they were 14 years old. Not that they show their age. Delaine has refurbished and repainted them and given them Select registrations — AD51 DLD and AD51 DLE — similar to those on the rest of the double-deck fleet.

The 20 bought new were delivered between 2000 and 2017. There are five B7TLs with East Lancs Vyking bodies, five B9TLs with East Lancs Olympus bodies (the first of these, exhibited on the bodybuilder's stand at the Euro Bus Expo show in 2006, was the first Olympus built), seven B9TLs with Wright Eclipse Gemini 2 bodies and three Euro6 B5TLs with Wright Gemini 3 bodies.

These choices reveal that although Delaine might be a small operator with the freedom to buy whatever it wants, it also likes to standardise as much as it can on vehicles it expects to keep for a full economic life. For that reason, when it resumed double-deck purchasing after Leyland stopped building the Atlantean, it held off purchasing the Olympian until the Volvo version — which it knew was in development — became available in 1993.

It began purchasing East Lancs bodies — initially to rebody Leyland Tiger single-deckers — after the Duple factory closed in 1989 and turned to Wrights from 2011 in the aftermath of a series of takeovers which amalgamated East Lancs with Optare, leading to the closure of its Blackburn factory and withdrawal from the body-on-chassis market. It was already familiar with Wrights' products, having purchased secondhand Volvo B10Bs with step-entrance Endurance bodies in 2003.

All three Gemini 3s have the 'classic' style front carried over from the Gemini 2, rather than the revised 'stealth' front introduced in 2014 when the new model went into volume production. Apart from any subjective view about the aesthetic appeal of the new design, with its sharper edges, at the time Delaine being situated in a gravel belt was also concerned about the potential replacement cost of its large curved drivers' windscreen. It managed to persuade the bodybuilder — like Delaine the Wrights Group is a family-owned business — to build the second and third to the same design as the first.

In this it may have been helped by Dublin Bus's insistence on also sticking with the 'classic' front, though the Delaine trio have the standard driver's windscreen rather than the bespoke angled version made only for Dublin.

With Delaine turning its attention next to renewing its single-deck fleet, it has mellowed its view of Wrights' 'stealth' front and has opted to incorporate it into the first of a possible eventual intake of six or seven Volvo B8RLEs with the Eclipse 3 body. Before placing the order for its first new single-decker in over 20 years, Ian and Anthony Delaine-Smith took themselves to Edinburgh for a close look at the similar vehicles built for Lothian Buses' East Coast Buses subsidiary in 2017. The Delaine bus is a standard length, at just over 12m, and allocated fleet number 164 in a series that started with the Model T Ford from 100 years earlier.

This careful approach to vehicle specification has also seen a gradual updating of the interior of Delaine buses, which still incorporate its own unique red tartan moquette pattern for upholstered seats and wood veneer side panels. Rather than adopting

bright yellow for hand poles, it complied with disability access requirements by switching from chrome to a contrasting colour best described as 'white aluminium'. Dashboards are black to minimise reflections at night.

Investment is not confined to buses and from June 2018 it replaced its Almex A90 ticket machines with Wayfarer equipment capable of processing contactless card transactions.

## Looking after the heritage

While continuing to invest in the company's future, the Delaine-Smith family also are immensely proud of its history and the role that its buses continue to play in the daily lives of the people of this part of south Lincolnshire.

They have established a charitable trust that is separate from the bus company and are creating a museum for it on part of the depot site in Bourne, a facility due to open for public visits from April 2019. Should the unthinkable happen and Delaine Buses is sold one day in the future or exists no more, the Delaine Heritage Trust, its museum and collection will be protected.

At the heart of the collection are four Leylands and a Volvo new to the company. The Leylands are rear entrance halfcab Titans — 45 (KTL 780), a Willowbrook-bodied PD2/20 new in 1956, and 50 (RCT 3), a rare Yeates-bodied PD3/1 delivered in 1960 — 72 (ACT 540L), a Northern Counties-bodied Atlantean AN68/2R new in 1973, and 100 (E100 AFW), a Duple Dominant bus-bodied Tiger single-decker new in 1987, the last of four delivered over a five-year period and the final Dominant body produced by Duple. The Volvo — the company's first in a now all-Volvo fleet — is East Lancs-bodied Olympian 116 (M1 OCT) new in 1995 and the first of six purchased between then and 1999.

They help chart the story of what the company purchased and when. The Yeates-bodied PD3 is one of two bought by Delaine and the only double-deckers that the Loughborough coachbuilder ever produced; the other one (new in 1959) survives in preservation in the Netherlands.

Delaine was one of few operators to buy Yeates bodies in quantity, becoming its fourth largest customer. Besides the two double-deckers, there were ten single-deckers — nine Bedford SBs and a still surviving Leyland Tiger Cub — bought between 1954 and 1964. The family story is that Hugh Delaine-Smith who often met socially with Yeates managing director Charles Yeates explained that he

ABOVE: *The museum collection includes this drawing produced by Yeates for the livery to be applied to 55 or 56, two Bedford SB5s new in the early 1960s with chassis modified by the coachbuilder to accommodate its Pegasus body with entrance ahead of the front axle.* Alan Millar

had to go to its rival next door Willowbrook as the company's next purchase would be a double-decker and Yeates did not build any. Out of that meeting arose a challenge that resulted the unique pair of PD3s.

Delaine bought an AEC on two occasions and in 1953 purchased a Strachans-bodied Regent III. That appears to have been enough to have given the manufacturer cause to believe it was in with a chance a few years later — around the time the Yeates-bodied PD3s were ordered — and a representative called with the proposition that the Lincolnshire independent might consider buying a couple of Routemasters.

The Delaine-Smith brothers are not sure how far these discussions progressed with their father, nor if any detailed specification was ever agreed for what might have been the only rear-entrance Routemasters built for service outside London. Much later on, in the 1990s, Delaine had its own Routemaster experience, operating as vehicle 113 in its chronological fleet numbering series former London Transport RM2059, on extended loan and painted in full fleet livery. It survives, once again a genuine red London bus.

The 1973 Atlantean saw 22 years' front line service before seeing out its final operational years on school services and was one of two bought new by Delaine — Willowbrook-bodied PDR1/2 60 from 1966 is restored and owned privately — and was one of comparatively few double-deckers ordered by independents in the 1970s. Delaine ordered both of its Atlanteans at the same time as Whippet Coaches in Cambridgeshire took near identical vehicles in an example of a little more purchasing power that in this case arose through the personal friendship between Hugh Delaine-Smith and Harry Lee whose

BELOW: *The workshop display includes coronation biscuit tins, a National Dried Milk tin, sticking plasters, pipe tobacco, a measuring tape and boxes of obsolete lamps and other spare parts.* Alan Millar

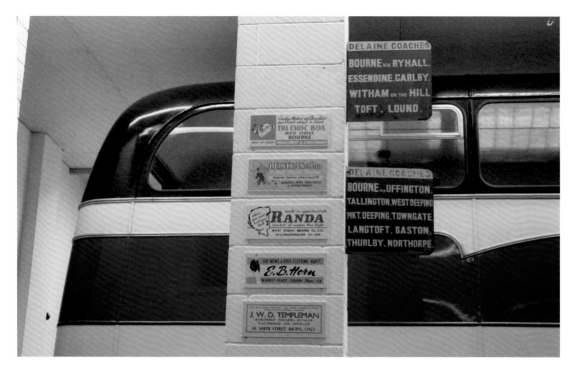

ABOVE: *Period advertisements and bus station signs in the museum alongside the Yeates-bodied PD3.* Alan Millar

family owned Whippet.

That friendship saw the two independents sometimes exchange vehicles, mostly from Delaine to Whippet, and it was on Harry Lee's recommendation that Delaine bought its first Duple Dominant bus bodies. After purchasing one of the first B58 coach chassis sold in Britain, he also tried to convince his friend in Lincolnshire that Volvo was the way forward, but Delaine remained loyal to Leyland until the marque was no longer available.

Besides these vehicles, the museum is being packed full of artefacts and displays that help tell the Delaine story. Some appear as wall decorations or as story boards within display cabinets, others in the recreation of a workshop and depot office.

These are objects that more ruthless and less sentimental organisations would have long since consigned to a skip. To several skips over several years. There are accounts ledgers, private hire bookings diaries, sketches of liveries for vehicles on order, timetable displays, destination blinds and boards, registration number plates from vehicles long departed, the wooden blocks used to create the traditional scroll fleetnames, plastic fleet name displays from 1960s coaches, old wheel trims, coachbuilders' 'on delivery' window stickers, seats salvaged from the Strachans-bodied Regent and an ex-Greater Manchester Atlantean, ticket machines and an impressive collection of photographs.

The workshop display includes obsolete lamps and drive belts, some still in their original wrappers, as well as more everyday items like old cigarette packets, tins of sticking plaster, biscuit barrels from the 1937 and 1953 coronations (the older one with a hole in the lid to hold a ball of string), even a tin of Rodine-branded rat poison.

The office, with Hugh Delaine-Smith's desk and chair, includes the inevitable ashtray as well as Bakelite phone with traditional dial and cord flex, a Burroughs adding machine and hand-cranked Gestetner duplicating machine that represented the cutting edge of multiple document copying before photocopiers became commonplace in the 1970s.

This collection, appealing to the memories of more than just bus enthusiasts, will also be an educational resource for the area and will open specially for group visits. It will open to the public one Saturday afternoon each month and for spring and autumn running days when the museum buses will operate a heritage service between Bourne and Stamford while selected visiting vehicles operate tours along sections of the route between Bourne and Rippingale; an opportunity to enjoy some motorbus industry heritage while also celebrating the survival and prosperity of the company that has fostered it over the past 100 years. ■

# More than madder

**Richard Walter** provides a flavour of what have been a very busy few years in the development of Lothian Buses, and shows that not all buses are in the city's traditional madder livery.

All photographs by the author.

ABOVE: *1002 (LXZ 5384) (formally BG61 SXR), is one of 50 extensively-refurbished ex-First London Wright Eclipse Gemini 2-bodied Volvo B9TLs which entered service with Lothian Buses in 2018 to accelerate the renewal of the fleet. It is crossing the tram tracks in Edinburgh's famous Princes Street, the hub of the city's tourist activity.*

E dinburgh has always had a reputation for having an excellent public transport system. The smart madder and white livery has existed through a number of organisational changes from the early days of Edinburgh Corporation Transport, followed by Lothian Region Transport from 1975 (when the livery was enhanced by a harlequin design for a few years) and then council-owned Lothian Buses which with a new swooped version of the traditional colours was to form part of an alliance with the Edinburgh Trams project under the umbrella of Transport for Edinburgh.

In addition to the operation of regular bus services, open-top tours became a major attraction over the years. Routes expanded out into Midlothian, East Lothian and West Lothian following deregulation in 1986, and the expanded operating area brought new challenges.

Throughout the years various ideas were tried including the route branding of certain services

and all-over advertising, not forgetting a long-term relationship with Edinburgh Zoo which has seen some examples of animal-themed liveries on routes 26 and 31 which serve the Zoo. There has also been a desire to try out various demonstrators including articulated buses, battery electric buses, and shorter vehicles for specific routes - the most recent being Optare Solos which were phased out during 2017-18.

Alexanders of Falkirk provided many of the buses over the years with the Wrightbus/Volvo combination being the first choice in more recent times. Whilst the fleet boasts a good number of single-deck buses, double-deckers have long been seen as the best way to transport people around the city and beyond. The disappearance of First Scotland East in Musselburgh and North Berwick saw Lothian Buses creating a new company - Lothian Country Buses - and taking over garages and routes during 2016.

Changes of management saw some significant alterations made from 2016 onwards with the formation of a family of connected companies. During 2017 in addition to the main bus operation (which uses the Lothian fleetname) passengers in East Lothian saw Lothian Country Buses develop into East Coast Buses, with the Lothian Country identity then being used on routes serving the people of Queensferry.

The popular Airlink airport service 100 had an image change during 2017, and two new airport services, 200 and 300, were created under the Skylink banner. Together with Edinburgh Bus Tours (comprising the City Sightseeing, Edinburgh Tour, Majestic Tour and 3 Bridges Tour identities) and the NightBus network the family was nearly complete. In the spring of 2018 a coach and private hire division was added, trading as Lothian Motorcoaches, in the terminology used in North America.

The liveries have settled on a standardised attractive new style. They are madder and white for the Lothian bus fleet, green and grey for East Coast Buses, green and cream for Lothian Country, blue and grey for Airlink and blue and white for Skylink. The coaches introduced in 2018 are grey.

With customer journeys on the increase, during 2017 Lothian invested £20.9million in 80 Euro 6 buses and six fully electric buses. Along with these new buses 50 extensively refurbished ex-First London Wright Eclipse Gemini 2-bodied Volvo B9TLs helped speed fleet replacement in 2018. ∎

ABOVE: *Freshly repainted in the latest style of livery at The Jewel is 959 (SN11 EAO), a Wright Eclipse Gemini 2-bodied Volvo B9TL which was one of several initially delivered in branded livery for service 5.*

ABOVE: *10106 (RIG 6496) (previously GN06 EVR) is one of seven Wright Eclipse Volvo B7RLEs bought second hand from Arriva Kent Thameside when East Coast Buses was set up in 2016. The bus is seen on Dalkeith town service 39 leaving the Midlothian Community Hospital.*

BELOW: *Pictured in the suburb of Morningside is Wright Eclipse Urban Volvo B7RLE 158 (SN57 DDA) on service 38 to the Royal Infirmary.*

LEFT: *Looking smart in its original Lothian Buses livery is Wright Eclipse Gemini Volvo B9TL 339 (SN59 BGE), outside the Western General Hospital on the cross-city 19 service from Granton to King's Road, Portobello.*

RIGHT: *Previously 796 with Lothian Buses, Wright Gemini Volvo B7TL 20796 (SN56 AEW) was one of seven additional buses required for East Coast Buses following disposal of Plaxton-bodied Dennis Tridents in 2017.*

*A line up of open-top Wright Gemini Volvo B5TL Euro 6 buses at their launch on 18 August 2016 at the Grassmarket. The lead vehicle, 234 (SJ16 CTX), is in Edinburgh Tour colours. Those behind are liveried for the Majestic Tour and City Sightseeing.*

BELOW: *Representing the Lothian Country fleet is Wright Gemini Volvo B9TL 929 (SN09 CVP) in Queensferry. The 43 and X43 provide a link from Queensferry to Edinburgh city centre.*

ABOVE: *The most recent Gemini 3s have glazed corners on the front of the upper deck but earlier vehicles, such as 2015 delivery 428 (SA15 VTF), had thick corner pillars. The Euro 6 Volvo B5TL is on North Bridge heading for Mayfield on service 3.*

BELOW: *10051 (SF17 VLX), one of 15 high-specification Wright Eclipse Urban 3-bodied Volvo B8RLE Euro 6 buses new to East Coast Buses, passes through Musselburgh on route 124 to North Berwick.*

ABOVE: *248 (SJ16 ZZP) is one of the open-top fleet of Wright Eclipse Volvo B5TL Euro 6s in Majestic Tour livery, here approaching Ocean Terminal where the Royal Yacht Britannia is berthed as a major tourist attraction.*

BELOW: *Representing an older open-top vehicle still in service is 219 (W632 PSX), a Dennis Trident with Plaxton President bodywork. During the summer of 2017, 219 and other open-toppers were loaned to East Coast Buses at weekends to duplicate on service 124. It seen at Levenhall, Musselburgh, returning from a journey to North Berwick.*

ABOVE: *Two Plaxton President-bodied Dennis Tridents are required to operate the 3 Bridges Tour to Queensferry and carry an orange and red livery. 651 (XIL 1484) (previously SK52 OHN) climbs from the pier at Queensferry with the Forth Bridge behind it.*

ABOVE LEFT: *When the relatively new Airlink double-deckers were replaced by new buses in a new livery in 2017, part of the 2015 batch of Wright Eclipse Volvo B5TL Euro 6s transferred to the new Skylink services. 436 (SA15 VTP) awaits passengers at Edinburgh Airport on service 200 which operates to Ocean Terminal on the opposite side of the city.*

ABOVE: *In the spring of 2018 Lothian Buses re-entered the coach business with five Volvo B11Rs with Plaxton Panther bodies.*

*New to Lothian Buses in 2017 were six Wright StreetAir electric buses which have charging stations at Central Garage. 287 (SK67 FLF) is seen with the impressive backdrop of Edinburgh Castle in December 2017.*

# The Pacific Northwest

**Michael Dryhurst** takes us on a road trip through both space and time in the USA and Canada where he finds many buses with British connections.

The Club Car of the 20th Century Limited. Cary Grant proffers Eva Marie Saint his business card. She studies it. "Roger O. Thornhill." She looks at him. "What's the 'O' for?" "Nothing..."
Eh, getting mixed-up with the specifics of my pacifics; that was one of the many classic lines from the movie North by North West.

But. The article heading here does not refer to an airline, a bus line, a railroad train nor a film. It is the

ABOVE: *In the California state capital, Sacramento, Sac RT, as it is dubbed locally, has been host to a number of demonstrators, including this Chance midibus, built under licence from Wrightbus of Ballymena. The bus was very popular with drivers, but no orders followed. Michael Dryhurst*

*In north-east California is the Sierra Nevada mountain range, the highest point of which is at some 9,000ft-plus, in El Dorado County, California. Descending from Echo Summit is Greyhound 5514, an MCI MC9, in all probability carrying a load of gamblers from the San Francisco Bay Area to the gambling Mecca of Stateline, Nevada. Nevada is one of only two US states where gambling is legal, the other being New Jersey. Michael Dryhurst*

ABOVE: *Eleven miles west of Sacramento is the university town of Davis, where the local transit operator Unitrans has a small fleet of ex-British double-deckers plus two ADL Enviro500s delivered new. This 1993 shot sees now-withdrawn RT1235 which was powered by a Leyland O.600 engine, and one of the two now long-gone ex-West Riding Daimler Fleetlines with Roe bodywork; this had an entrance on the US nearside, the rear-engine layout and length making this possible. Note the ventilator inserted into the front dome; in the summer Davis gets very hot...* Michael Dryhurst

generic name for an area of north America which covers the US states of Oregon and Washington plus the Canadian province of British Columbia, and as writers are wont to do, I've taken licence here, and have included also Northern California, for two reasons:

1) Northern California supplies all of the water consumed by Southern California (Los Angeles

actually was built in a desert) and resents it dearly, seeking frequently to become a separate state but more importantly to the bus enthusiast, 2) it has much of bus transport interest.

So we'll take a leisurely trip through the region, starting from the foothills of the Sierra Nevada (where once lived your author) to the flat of Vancouver Island, the home of Victoria, the capital of the Canadian province of British Columbia. All of which is a considerable distance from Placerville (pronounced Plasserville), the county seat of El

BELOW: *To the south of Sacramento is Amador County where beside California highway 88 had stood for some ten years this White, built as a school bus. Having languished here for a decade, summer and winter (very hot in the summer, very wet in the winter), perhaps the owner was somewhat optimistic with the asking price? It disappeared in early 2006.* Michael Dryhurst

BELOW: *Photographed in a mobile home park in Vallejo, east of San Francisco, is this ex-Western National Bristol FLF6B, still displaying its original Devon registration, AUO 514B. It had been driven from Chicago to Vallejo on Interstate 80, some 2,100 miles, on the way crossing both the Rockies and the Sierra Nevada mountain ranges.* Michael Dryhurst

ABOVE: *In the East Bay of San Francisco lies the territory of Alameda County, the main operator there being AC Transit. This shows two of its once large fleet of General Motors' TDH-series New Look transit buses (aka Fishbowl), by far the best-selling vehicle of its type, built in both Canada and the USA. And possibly the best-looking transit bus to be produced in North America.* Michael Dryhurst collection

ABOVE: *In 1995 trams (streetcars) returned to the main artery of downtown San Francisco, Market Street, and for operation of the F-line, Muni had been accumulating PCC streetcars from all over the USA, to add to its own stock of such preserved vehicles. Seen here on The Embarcadero at the Ferry Terminus is Muni 1057, a 1948 PCC built by the St Louis Car Co for the Philadelphia Transportation Co. Purchased by Muni in 1992, it was refurbished in 1993 by Morrison-Knudsen and as an homage to the type, painted in the livery of Cincinnati Street Railway Co. The car beside the PCC is the former Blackpool Tramways 228, a 1934-built English Electric 'boat' donated by Blackpool to Muni in 1984; another boat donated here is the former 233, from the Lancastrian Transport Trust.* Michael Dryhurst

ABOVE: *After having been filming in Japan, your author first set foot in the USA in 1969 at San Francisco, where at Fisherman's Wharf he encountered an ex-Bristol Omnibus Co KSW6B which had been converted to open-top by Smith's Coaches of Reading. It carries both Californian and UK licence plates.* Michael Dryhurst

Dorado County and the base of its transit system.

El Dorado Transit doesn't operate what we'd have historically termed stage carriage services. However, from virtually over most of the county it does operate scheduled commuter services into Sacramento, the state capital and thus the area of major employment, such that commuter services are run into Sac from all points of the compass by ten different transit operators. Then in the capital itself is Sacramento Regional Transit known to all and sundry as Sac RT; the regional bit is a misnomer as its operations are confined to the city and its suburbs. Sac RT operates both buses and light rail, the latter having been enlarged considerably since its inauguration in the late 1990s.

A quick run west on I-80 over the Causeway brings us to Davis, its university being the most famous veterinary institute west of the Mississippi. However,

ABOVE: *Moving into Oregon, the area around the state capital of Salem is renowned for cherry-growing (the witches are in Salem, Maine...). In Oregon, the Salem transit system is dubbed The Cherriots, the word a mix of cherries and chariots. The fleet comprised a number of the short wheelbase RTS bus, by then not a GMC product but produced by MCI, in Roswell, New Mexico.* Michael Dryhurst

arguably much more important than that is the University's own transit system, Unitrans. Operated in conjunction with the City of Davis its fleet includes six UK buses, four of which are ex-London Transport stock, namely RTs 742, 2819, 3123 and 4735, all of these now ranging age-wise from some 64 to 70 years old, based on their bonnet numbers; only the ghost of Aldenham knows their true ages.

All of these buses have been retrofitted with new powertrains, including RT2819, converted to run on CNG. Additional to the RTs is a brace of ADL Enviro500s, which are much-liked and Unitrans was expecting a further brace in the autumn of 2018, presumably to be built at the ADL facility in the USA, at Nappanee, Indiana. Whether this results in any RTs being withdrawn is a wait-and-see exercise... In fact, it won't. They'll survive until state agency Caltrans decrees 'No!'

Davis is served also by YoloBus and Vacaville Transit.

Continuing west on I-80 (which runs from New York City to San Francisco more-or-less per the famous Route 66), are passed Vacaville (the transit system of which once was operated by Stagecoach), Fairfield and Vallejo, both of which have their own transit systems then across Carquinez Bridge over the top end of San Francisco Bay, into a number of counties which are known generically as

The Bay Area, with each administration operating its own transit system, from very large, to minuscule, the largest and the most interesting of which is the San Francisco Municipal Railway, aka Muni.

Muni operates buses, light rail, streetcars (trams) and trolleybuses but its territory is limited to the city and county of San Francisco although such is its variety of vehicles and operations it warrants a book devoted solely to itself. Like many transit agencies in North America, Muni has a heritage fleet of all types once operated; in fact, the whole of the streetcar F-Line operating now between Castro and Fisherman's Wharf is maintained with heritage vintage cars. The most-used are either refurbished PCCs or ex-Milan Peter Witt trams. While the PCCs carry liveries associated with the major users of the type, the Peter Witt cars retain their Italian municipal orange colour.

The bus and trolleybus fleets comprise both articulated and rigid vehicles, the former being mostly Gillig and New Flyer. Gillig is a local manufacturer, based in the East Bay city of Hayward, although for many years not receiving any business from Muni. Now that the Czech-derived Skoda trolleys are being withdrawn rapidly, the trolleybus fleet soon will be 100 per cent New Flyer, the Canadian-based company which is now the sole builder of trolleybuses in North America, but under the strict terms of the Buy America policy.

BELOW: *This AEC Regent III with Weymann body was originally RLH3 in the London Transport fleet. It was withdrawn in March 1965, passing to Passenger Vehicle Sales (a forerunner of today's dealership, Ensign) and thence to its affiliate, Super Coaches of Upminster, which numbered it RLH531 indicating 53-seater number 1. It was exported to California in 1968.* Michael Dryhurst

*Reputedly, San Francisco's Muni operates on some of the world's steepest trolleybus routes, as witnessed here as New Flyer E900 5294 climbs up from the Marina district and crosses Broadway, with yet another hill to come before is reached the summit. Michael Dryhurst*

ABOVE: *Oregon and Washington are separated by the Columbia River, in the latter state Seattle being the major city, but not the capital. Currently, Seattle Metro and its successor operate a mixed fleet of buses, light rail and trolleybuses. Completed in 1990 was the Third Street Transit Tunnel but as is seen with the track visible at the top right, the tunnel was intended always as a light rail facility. The trolleybuses used were Italian Breda bi-mode artics, 236 of them, which outside of the tunnel operated in diesel mode. 5043, seen here in May 1991, is below the Financial District. Michael Dryhurst.*

Touted recently so vociferously by President Trump, in the case of the bus-building industry the Buy America policy allows for vehicles used on both commuter and transit services to qualify for federal funding of up to 80 per cent of their cost but they must have been assembled in the USA and 70 per cent of their build content must be of US manufacture, which for foreign companies such as ADL, New Flyer and Nova Bus accounts for the setting-up by them of production facilities within the USA.

Interestingly, though, not every operator takes advantage of the federal funding. Back in the late 1990s, Bay Area operator AC Transit bought a large fleet of Van Hool buses, both artic and rigid, produced entirely in Belgium and thus not eligible for a red cent of federal funding; the whole was financed by money raised by the operator. Currently, AC Transit has on order 15 ADL Enviro500 double-deckers, to be built at the ADL plant in Indiana, with an option on another five. Muni has evaluated an ADL Enviro500 but no orders have been placed – yet.

Other transit agencies operating into downtown San Francisco are AC Transit from the east and north-east Bay Area; Golden Gate Transit (which agency also controls the Golden Gate Bridge and the Trans Bay ferries to Marin County) from the north; and Sam Mateo Transit (SamTrans) from the south.

If and when staying in San Francisco (and do not ever refer to it as Frisco, SF or San Fran; you'll be lynched. The citizens refer to it always and only as San Francisco. You have been warned...) you must sample the cable cars, but do so early morning or late evening, as the three lines get swamped in-between hours. And not all of the cars are old. As they get withdrawn they are replaced by new vehicles but to the traditional designs; currently the age of the cars on the California line ranges from 1906 to 2003, those on the Hyde and Powell lines from 1893 to 1994.

Leaving the city via US Highway 101, it's over the Golden Gate Bridge and at Novato we cross to Vallejo and I-80, to Vacaville and north to the I-5. Built

ABOVE: *Back in the early 1990s, the Vancouver Gray Line franchisee operated three VRT Bristols, one ex-Western SMT, another ex-Brighton Hove & District/Southdown and this example, ex-Western National. Like the Lodekka illustrated earlier, the VRT still carries its Devon number plate, OTA 292G. On these buses a four-leaf door was provided on the UK offside, aft of the stairs.* Michael Dryhurst

in the 1960s, I-5 snakes from the Mexican border to that of Canada.

When living in Shingle Springs twice I drove thence to Vancouver via I-5 and Canada 99, a drive of some 1,100 miles each way. On entering Oregon the I-5 crests the 4,167ft Siskiyou Summit and drops down into Ashland, the local transport provider there sporting the wonderful name of The Rogue Valley Transportation District, at which time it operated Bluebird short-wheelbase buses and some 30ft GMC Fishbowls, both now but a memory.

Onward, via I-5, which Interstate bisects the city of Portland, Oregon, on a lengthy viaduct. Once

an operator of a large trolleybus system, these days the main transit provider is TriMet, the name of which represents the three counties its buses serve. Additionally, there is C-Transit, serving the outer suburbs, MAX, the city's extensive light rail system and the downtown Portland Streetcar, which operates snazzy light rail vehicles.

Okay; back on to I-5, to Seattle, Washington. Although the state's capital is Olympia, Seattle is the largest city therein, and with a wealth of public transport interest.

The Seattle trolleybus system was inaugurated in 1940 and currently operates some 170-plus vehicles, mostly of New Flyer manufacture. Back in 1990 was opened the Third Avenue Transit Tunnel, for which was purchased some 238 Italian Bredabus articulated hybrid vehicles, operated in the tunnel as trolleybuses while the hybrid part was the diesel engine which propelled them on the freeway. When completed, the tunnel incorporated track for light rail, and now are gone the trolleybuses, replaced by light rail vehicles and hybrid buses.

Also gone is the waterfront heritage tram line, operated by vintage trams purchased from Melbourne, Oz. But while some of the cars have been sold, a

BELOW: *There are two operators of the very popular ADL Enviro500 in the Seattle area, these being Community Transit and King County Metro Transit. Seen in downtown Seattle is Community Transit 10815, which operator has on order further examples of this type.* Roger Davies

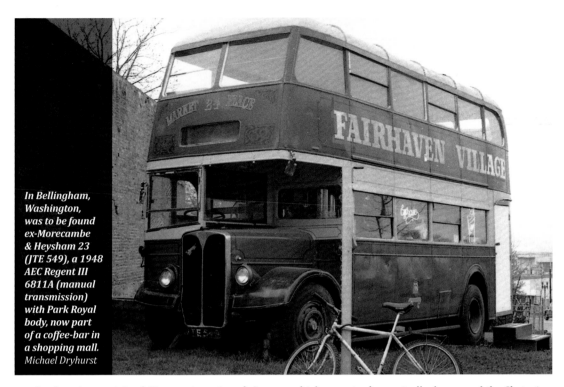

In Bellingham, Washington, was to be found ex-Morecambe & Heysham 23 (JTE 549), a 1948 AEC Regent III 6811A (manual transmission) with Park Royal body, now part of a coffee-bar in a shopping mall. *Michael Dryhurst*

number have been retained. Hope springs eternal...?

Back on I-5 up to Blaine and the border (and I bet no longer to be found in Bellingham is that ex-Morecambe Park Royal-bodied AEC Regent III converted to an espresso bar...?). Blaine is on the US side of the border, where whatever the state of the tank, fill it up as gasoline is much more expensive in Canada. I-5 finishes at the border. From here on it's Canada Highway 99.

Vancouver. The largest city in British Columbia; but not the capital. Transport provided by what was BC Transit, renamed now to Coast Mountain Bus Co, which operates buses, trolleybuses and the Skytrain metro system. Presumably for geological reasons, BC Transit didn't tunnel for a subway but built high, the trains running mostly on viaducts, giving spectacular views over the city and suburbs, while its trolleybus system has something in common with that of Muni: four-track overhead. In San Francisco it's on Market Street; in Vancouver, Hastings Street, to permit the operation of an express trolleybus route. Bliss!

All trolleybuses are of New Flyer manufacture, a mix of artics and rigids and with most motorbuses from the same Canadian company. On demonstration recently have been two ADL Enviro500 buses, and this has resulted for an order for 32 for 2019 delivery.

Pacific Coach Lines many moons ago had a fleet of Western Star coaches, a Canadian company which was purchased eventually by Daimler-Benz and merged into the German company's

LEFT: *Many US and Canadian transit agencies possess a heritage fleet of preserved vehicles. This is one such vehicle, formerly trolleybus 798 in the fleet of Seattle Transit and in use still on enthusiast charters. It is of Brill manufacture. Roger Davies*

ABOVE: *Interestingly, of the three western seaboard trolleybus systems, two have sections of street equipped with four-lane overhead, Market Street in San Francisco and Hastings Street in Vancouver. On the latter thoroughfare, two BC Transit New Flyer E800 trolleybuses await the off, with that on the right being on the express line.* Michael Dryhurst

Freightliner operation based in Portland, Oregon, at which time it ceased Western Star coach production. Any road, PCL operates a daily service to Vancouver Island, now using Canadian-built Prevost (pronounced Prevo) coaches. Prevost is part of the Volvo group.

Vancouver Island....Victoria; the provincial capital. Given its one-time content of ex-UK buses, perhaps it should have been re-named Valhalla Island... Alas, now with few ex-UK buses still operating, but on the occasions I visited were to be found ex-London RTs and RTLs, and buses emanating from Bristol Omnibus, Crosville, Derby Corporation, East Midland, Fishwick, Midland General, St Helens Corporation, Southdown, Trent, West Bridgford, West Yorkshire Road Car and Western National.

But all is not UK-lost. BC Transit on Vancouver Island operates a mix of some 181 ADL and Dennis buses; 69 Enviro500 and a total of 112 Dart and Dart SLF buses. Keeping the flag flying?

Well, I guess that's it. Hope you enjoyed the journey.

In conclusion I must thank old friends for contributing info and photographs, namely Paul Bateson, Roger Davies, Mike Isles and Bob Martin, plus acknowledgement is given to these publications:

*Bus World Encyclopaedia of Buses*, Stauss Publications, 1988.

*Postwar second-hand British buses in North America*, PSV Circle, 1986.

*On Track*, Rick Laubscher, Heyday Books/Market Street Railway, 2014. ∎

BELOW: *The Gray Line franchisee in Victoria, British Columbia, purchased two Weymann-bodied lowheight PDR1 Atlanteans which had originated with renowned independent Fishwick of Leyland. One is greeting tourists from Port Angeles, USA, from the legendary vessel Princess Marguerite, operated by Canadian Pacific Railways.* Mike Isles

All photographs by the author.

# Go-Ahead in East Anglia

The Go-Ahead group has been running buses in East Anglia since 2010.
**Geoff Mills** illustrates a selection.

ABOVE: *Anglian Bus of Beccles was purchased by Go-Ahead in 2012, and closed in November 2017 when its operations were absorbed by Konectbus. Among the more unusual buses in the Anglian fleet was this Caetano-bodied MAN 18.270, 105 (WX62 HFU), operating on compressed natural gas. It was one of six delivered towards the end of 2012 and is seen in Lowestoft in 2013. The gas buses were transferred to Plymouth Citybus in 2016.*

LEFT: *In 2012 Go-Ahead transferred 13 Volvo B7TLs with Plaxton President bodies from its London fleet to Chambers, where they replaced elderly step-entrance double-deckers. New in 2000, 572 (W489 WGH) is seen in Church Street, Lavenham, in 2017. The attractive livery features branding for the route between Bury St Edmunds, Sudbury and Colchester.*

ABOVE: *Anglian bought two new Scania K230UB with Scania's own 46-seat bodywork in 2011. 454 (YT11 LVF) is seen in Castle Meadows, Norwich when new.*

ABOVE: *When London turned against articulated buses this Mercedes-Benz Citaro which had been part of Go-Ahead's London General fleet was transferred to Konectbus in 2011, at which point it was just three years old. 802 (BD57 WCZ) is seen in Norwich in 2014 operating a park-and-ride service. Konectbus was Go-Ahead's first East Anglian acquisition in 2010.*

BELOW: *Another inter-group transfer to Konectbus was this 78-seat East Lancs-bodied Dennis Trident which came from Brighton & Hove. 724 (W824 NNJ) was new in 2000 and joined the Konectbus fleet in 2013.*

ABOVE: *This Tempo X1200 was originally an Optare demonstrator in 2005. 414 (YJ55 BLX) was then bought by Anglian Bus and was later moved to Konectbus. It is seen in King's Lynn.*

BELOW: *Chambers was another 2012 acquisition by Go-Ahead. This ADL Enviro200, 261 (EY57 FZE), had been new to Hedingham in 2007 and was transferred to the Chambers fleet in 2015.*

ABOVE: *At the start of 2012 Konectbus took delivery of five ADL Enviro400s. This is a 2015 view, showing 609 (SN61 CZZ) with Konect Express route branding for the service from Norwich to Dereham and Toftwood.*

BELOW: *This B10BLE with Alexander ALX300 body started life in 1998 as a Volvo demonstrator and was purchased by Hedingham in the following year. 480 (S376 MVP) is leaving Colchester bus station for Halstead in 2015.*

ABOVE: *Hedingham's first new double-decker, in 1999, was L300 (S300 XHK), a long-wheelbase Volvo Olympian with 87-seat lowheight Alexander body. This is a 2014 view in Westlands, Colchester.*

BELOW: *Probably the best-known name in the Go East Anglia operations is Hedingham, purchased in 2012. This 2000 Dennis Dart, L394 (X346 YGU), was transferred from Brighton & Hove in 2012, and is seen in Colchester High Street the following year, still in its previous owner's livery which was a reasonable match for Hedingham's own colours.*

# The game of the name

**Gavin Booth** explores the art of naming bus models.

*All photographs by the author.*

t used to be easy. Leyland front-engined double-deckers were all Titans and AEC's equivalent was the Regent. Guy apparently used Arab for everything and Daimler was boring because it only used letters and numbers. That was in the 1950s when life seemed to be simple for this fledgling bus spotter armed only with a dog-eared Ian Allan *ABC Buses and Coaches*.

We relied on radiator badges to know which company had built the chassis, but not all of them told you much more than that. Daimler didn't even see the need to display its name; like its cars, the buses had that distinctive fluted top to the radiator that surely said it all. But what model was it? That was a different matter.

Bodybuilders? We relied on internal metal or plastic plates or sometimes transfers to identify the manufacturer; my *ABC* told me that some bodybuilders gave their models names, but these were rarely if ever displayed.

Observant passengers might notice the chassis builder's logo on the front end, or the bodybuilder's name somewhere inside, but did they know that they were travelling on an Arab or a Titan chassis, or indeed inside a Metro-Cammell Aurora or Orion

ABOVE: *MCW had a virtual monopoly on 'Metro' model names in the 1980s. A 1986 London United Metrobus crosses Kingston Bridge.*

body? And did they care? As a schoolboy I knew that the buses taking me to school were Leylands – it said so on the front – and a plate on the stair wall told me that the bodies were built in Birmingham by the impressive sounding Metropolitan-Cammell Carriage & Wagon company. But I only knew the Titan and Orion bits from the *ABC* – 2s 6d (12½p) well spent.

BELOW: *The Swift was one of the last new chassis introduced by AEC. This East Kent example carries AEC but not Swift badging, and the Alexander bodywork is of the W type as the company had almost reached the end of the alphabet. Leyland resurrected the Swift name for a midibus in 1987.*

ABOVE: *An example of the integral Scania OmniCity operating for Arriva Scotland West in Glasgow in 2009.*

Some manufacturers took what might seem to be the easy way out by avoiding names and sticking to model codes that were sometimes easy for teenage bus spotters to crack. So once we knew that a Daimler CVG6 was a Commercial Victory with a Gardner 6LW engine, we could deduce what a 5LW-engined CVG5 or a Daimler-engined CVD6 was, though CCG6 and CSG6 baffled us for a while until we worked out that these had Constant-mesh or Synchromesh gearboxes. Daimler rarely gave models names, but its 1951-introduced underfloor-engined chassis was the Freeline, its hugely successful 1960 rear-engined double-decker was the Fleetline and the rather less successful 1962 rear-engined single-deck the Roadliner.

Bristol had a similar system, so the LD6G was a Lodekka with a Gardner 6LW engine and an LS5G

a Light Saloon with a Gardner 5HLW engine. The Lodekka name was widely known and used, while the Light Saloon, Medium Weight, Small Underfloor, Small Capacity, Rear Engine and Vertical Rear (alias LS, MW, SU, SC, RE and VR) were typically known by their initials.

But then it all changed. Chassis manufacturers and even bodybuilders recognised that applying names to their products was the way forward – even though they rarely displayed these names so the only people who knew them were the manufacturers, a few people at bus company head offices – and of course the bus spotters.

London Transport understood the value of a good name and coined Routemaster for its trolleybus-replacement fleet. Where previously its buses were known by type codes whose origins enthusiasts still disagree over, this clever name caught the public imagination to such an extent that any double-decker

LEFT: *Leyland left nobody in any doubt about the model name or the company's credentials on this preserved 1929 Tiger.*

RIGHT: *Leyland's fine chrome and enamel badges like this pouncing Royal Tiger graced the fronts of many of its models in the 1950s and 1960s.*

ABOVE: *Optare burst on to the bus scene in 1985 and produced a range of attractive and innovative designs like the 1988 Delta, built on DAF SB220 chassis. This example is working for Edinburgh Transport in 1994.*

RIGHT: *Alexander Dennis and BYD – Build Your Dreams – co-operated to produce this pure-electric model, with Enviro200-style bodywork and badged as a BYD. Batches of these are in service in London, as here with Go-Ahead's London General fleet, at London Bridge station when new in 2016.*

with an engine at the front and an entrance at the back tends to be described as a Routemaster, even when we bus spotters know it patently isn't.

Lodekka was another great name from this era. Bristol and Eastern Coach Works devised this practical lowheight double-decker that avoided the awkward sunken gangway of previous generations of lowbridge buses and where previously its models were known by initials, with the Lodekka they came up with a name that caught on, and even appeared on the front grilles of later models. When other chassis builders came up with similar models, they followed Bristol's lead with the 'Lo' bit of their names – so we got the Loline from Dennis, the Lowlander from Leyland/Albion, but the Bridgemaster and Renown from AEC. And ranking alongside Lodekka in the great names category is Solo (so low) chosen by Optare for its best-selling midibus model.

Some of these names were so good that decades later they have been resurrected. East Lancs had a Lowlander and a Lolyne, Wrightbus a Renown, and Plaxton offers a Cheetah, Leopard, Panther and Panther Cub, previously inhabitants of the Leyland Zoo.

Observant readers will have noticed the spelling difference between Dennis's Loline and the East Lancs Lolyne, and East Lancs produced a series of mis-spelt bodies with that distinctive 'y' – the Cityzen, Flyte, Hyline, Myllennium, Pyoneer, Spryte and Vyking. These were sometimes subtle variations on a broadly similar design, so much so that it became difficult to identify them accurately. No such problem with the best-known 'y' type – the Alexander Y type single-deck body that was in production from 1961 to 1982. Alexander simply worked through the alphabet from the A type double-decker to the single-deck Z type developed for BET Group orders, and apart from a brief period in the 1990s when it coined names for single-deck bodies, it has stuck with numbers and letters ever since.

In 1996 Alexander turned to designations that indicated the size of the body - the ALX100 minibus, the ALX200 midibus, the ALX300 full-size single-decker, the ALX400 for two-axle double-deckers and the ALX500 for three axle double-deckers. More

LEFT: *The Alexander Dennis Enviro400 body range was introduced in 2006. This is a Stagecoach Cambridge 2007 delivery in park-and-ride livery.*

the Cub, Cheetah, Lion and Lioness. And Leyland went on to expand its zoo with Leopards, Lynxes, Panthers and Panther Cubs for its single-deck range, while its double-deckers stuck to legend and mythology, with Titans, Atlanteans and Olympians. Metro-Cammell also turned to Roman and Greek mythology with its Aurora and Orion double-deck bodies and its Apollo, Jason and Hermes single-deckers – though if you can identify a steel-built Apollo from an alloy Hermes or a knocked-down Jason for export markets, you're doing better than me.

Identifying different chassis types became easier when exposed radiators gave way to full fronts, with more of a blank canvas to display name badges. Even Daimler cast aside its anonymity and displayed the company name. But the best were the chunky Leyland chrome and enamel badges used to identify models like the Royal Tiger, Tiger Cub, Leopard and Atlantean with roaring Tigers and Leopards, cute Cubs and Atlas with the world on his shoulders. These revived memories of Leyland's pictorial badging of the 1930s.

Finding a name for a bus chassis or body is not easy, as I discovered in the 1990s while doing some work with Alexander. Many of the best names are

ABOVE: *The Alexander Dennis ALX300 was developed as a lighter-weight full-size single-decker. A Stagecoach 2006 example is seen in Winchester in 2008 in park-and-ride colours.*

recently, Alexander Dennis products have carried Enviro names – so the Enviro200 is the midi-size single-decker and so on. Sometimes these carry extra letters – the Enviro400H is a hybrid, the Enviro400 City is a variation largely aimed at London customers, and for a while reworked E200s and E400s were known as MMC – Major Model Change.

For years several of the major manufacturers had relied on families of model names that were applied to every chassis of a particular type. So while there was little similarity between AEC's 1929 double-decker and its 1968 equivalent, they were always Regents – and it was the same with Leyland's Titan. AEC had gone for 'R' names for its bus range – Regal, Regent, Renown, Ranger – Leyland had gone for 'T' names – Tiger, Titan, Titanic – as well as animals like

BELOW: *The Alexander Dennis Enviro400 double-deck range was updated in 2014 with what was known as the MMC version – Major Model Change. This is a gas-powered Reading Buses 2017 Enviro400CBG when new.*

ABOVE: *Alexander Dennis has built the gas-powered Enviro300SG on Scania K270UB chassis, as here with Reading Buses in 2016.*

ABOVE: *When the Wright Eclipse body is mounted on a Volvo B7LA articulated chassis it becomes the Eclipse Fusion. This First Aberdeen version is seen in 2014.*

in reserve for car manufacturers and hours spent poring over a dictionary in these pre-Google days resulted in Dash, for the midibus body, Strider for the big single-decker and Sprinter for the minibus. And later, when the R type double-deck got a makeover Alexander treated it to the name Royale.

Alexander went down the route of keeping a single type designation for each body style whatever the length, height or chassis underneath. Unlike Wright, which burst into the bodybuilding mainstream in the 1990s and which coined some wonderful names for its single-deck products. These started simply with their Endeavour and Endurance bodies but as the business grew, so did the complexity of the names. So similar-looking bodies on different chassis carried different names: the Axcess-ultralow on Scania L113, the Axcess Floline on Scania L94, the Liberator on Volvo B10L, the Renown on Volvo B10BLE, the Commander on the DAF SB200, the Crusader on Dennis Dart and Volvo B6LE, the Cadet on DAF/VDL

BELOW: *Operating for Translink's Metro fleet in Belfast in 2011, a Scania L94UB with Wright Solar bodywork.*

SB120 – and to complicate matters the SB120/Cadet was sold as the Volvo Merit when Volvo lacked a midi chassis of its own.

Wright simplified its names – well, a bit – with its Millennium range, launched in 1999. The solar eclipse at the time influenced its policy, so the Solar was a single-deck Scania and the Eclipse a single-deck Volvo. If it was a VDL SB200 it was a Pulsar and if they were articulated buses, the word Fusion was added. When Wright moved successfully into the double-deck body market in 2001, its body was the Gemini – twin decks – and in spite of major changes to the styling, still is, except when it was mounted on a VDL DB250 chassis, when it became the Pulsar Gemini. Or of course when it's a StreetDeck, from the range of integral buses built entirely by Wrightbus, in the same family as the StreetLite small bus, the StreetAir electric bus, and the original Street, the 2005 StreetCar artic developed in conjunction

BELOW: *The family resemblance is obvious in this 2005 view of two First Glasgow Volvos, a 2004 B7TL/Gemini double-deck and a 2001 B7L/Eclipse single-deck.*

ABOVE: *The Olympus introduced a sharper look to the East Lancs body range. A 2007 Cardiff Bus Olympus on Scania N230UD chassis in 2010.*

with FirstBus. And of course Wrightbus developed the New Routemaster for Transport for London – initially boringly known by Transport for London as the New Bus for London, and then more popularly and certainly unofficially as the Borismaster after Boris Johnson when he was Mayor of London.

East Lancs had a similarly complicated range of names. In addition to the 'y' types already mentioned, there was the MaxCi and European on

Scania chassis, the Olympus double-deck, the three-axle Nordic double-deck on Volvo, the OmniDekka in conjunction with Scania, the Esteem and Kinetic single-deckers, and the one and only Kinetic+ double-deck on MAN chassis.

Dennis went for names based on sharp things – hence the Arrow, Dart, Javelin and Lance – but also came up with D words – Dominator, Domino, Dorchester and Dragon.

Dominator is a good example of model names that were often intended to indicate some sort of superiority. Duple and Plaxton competed head-to-head for coach business with names that indicated their ambitions. So while Duple was Dominant and boasted a Commander, Plaxton went for Supreme and also tautograms (Google it, I did) like Paragon, Paramount, Premiere, President, Prestige, and Prima. Before World War 2 Morris Commercial had built the Imperial – but had also, perhaps unwisely given the political situation in the mid-1930s, offered the Dictator. Leyland's Titanic, introduced just 15 years after the sinking of the *Titanic*, may also have been a

LEFT: *The stylish Wright StreetCar artic was evolved for FirstBus on Volvo B7LA chassis – the first Wright model name with a 'Street' prefix. This 2007 First Leeds StreetCar is seen when new.*

ABOVE: *MAN produced its first double-decker for the UK market in 2006. Based on the ND243 chassis, the prototype – and only one built – was bodied by East Lancs as the Kinetic+, incorporating a standard MAN front end. It is seen operating for Reading Buses in 2007.*

rare error of judgement.

Superiority in battle is reflected in names chosen by Guy (Warrior, Victory), Willowbrook and Wright (Crusader), Albion (Valiant) and Commer (Avenger). Wildlife is another recurring theme. In addition to Leyland's Zoo there were the Falcon and Dragon (Dennis), AEC's (and Leyland's) Swift, and Plaxton's Beaver and Pointer.

Place names have provided fruitful inspiration for bus manufacturers, so Albion had its Aberdonian, Guy its Wulfrunian, Caetano a whole list of Portuguese towns and cities, Dennis the Dorchester, Plaxton the Derwent and Roe and Ward went for the Dalesman. The Aberdonian was a more basic

Leyland Tiger Cub, and the citizens of Aberdeen, Aberdonians, are renowned for their apparent thrift. A Wulfrunian is a native of Wolverhampton, where Guy chassis were built.

Manufacturers who recognised that buses are often urban animals, coined names that reflected where their products would be working. MCW had its Metrobus, Metroliner, Metropolitan, Metrorider and Metro-Scania; Optare its CityPacer, MetroDecker, MetroCity and MetroRider (note the capital R introduced when Optare acquired the rights to build MCW's Metrorider); Wrightbus has its Street variants; Iveco the TurboCity; UVG the UrbanStar; Wright the Urbanranger; Scania its OmniCity, OmniDekka and OmniTown, and Volvo its Citybus.

And when the pool of names dries up, bus manufacturers can emulate the car manufacturers and turn to made-up names, usually names that work well in different countries. So Optare had its Alero, Prisma, Vecta and Versa, and Plaxton its Centro.

Bedford stuck to initials, except for the 1984 Venturer. Seddon tended to call everything a Pennine, rather as Guy used Arab for a range of different models. Volvo came to the UK in 1973 with the B58, succeeded by the B10M (Bus, 10-litre engine, Mid-mounted) and still uses this system for current models like the B5TL (Bus, 5-litre, Transverse engine, Low) and the B8RLE (Bus, 8-litre,

BELOW: *Scania and East Lancs combined to produce the OmniDekka on the N94UD chassis. A 2006 Transdev Sovereign example at Golders Green, London, in 2009.*

ABOVE: *The integral Optare MetroDecker was introduced in 2014 and this demonstrator was working with Go North East in Newcastle in 2017.*

Rear-engined, Low-entry). But it carried on with the Olympian name when it inherited that successful model from Leyland, and applied the Citybus name to its underfloor-engined double-decker. Its other named chassis was the Ailsa, recognising that the development work on this latter-day front-engined double-decker was carried out by its dealer, Ailsa Trucks.

There are themes too in the names of manufacturers. Most are purely geographical (Albion, Bedford, Bristol, East Lancs, Leyland, Northern Counties) or based on the names of their founders (Alexander, Caetano, Daimler, Dennis, Ford, Guy, Plaxton, Weymann, Wright). Initials reflect a merger of interests (MCW is Metro-Cammell Weymann) or just a straightforward and fairly pedestrian description (AEC is the Associated Equipment Company). My favourite initials are those of the Chinese battery electric bus manufacturer BYD, which stands for Build Your Dreams.

As I was completing this article, I was momentarily excited to learn that the Egyptian manufacturer MCV had launched a new single-deck bus body called – I thought – the Évora, presumably named after the UNESCO World Heritage town in the south of Portugal that I had visited on many occasions. But no. The new model is the eVoRa, part of a family of eVo-prefixed names that includes the eVolution, the double-deck eVoSeti – Seti was an Egyptian pharaoh just as the Ra in eVoRa was the ancient Egyptian sun god.

Oh, and did you know that Volvo is Latin for 'I roll'? I knew the Latin I studied at school would come in useful one day! ■

BELOW: *Optare's Solo (so low) is a highly successful midibus model in the UK and overseas. A Preston Bus Optare Solo SR is seen in Preston in 2015.*

# A NORTH YORKSHIRE HOLIDAY

**Mike Greenwood** travels back in time, to a 1971 summer holiday centred on Whitby.

D o you recall those industrial holiday fortnights when a town's industry would substantially close down for two weeks so that a high proportion of the workforce could take their annual summer holiday?

In my home town of Leicester the industry shutdown coincided each year with the first two weeks of July. Whilst car ownership was rapidly gaining

BELOW: *Howlett's of Quorn used its 45-seat Plaxton-bodied Bedford VAM70 31 (MNR 833F) as the regular allocated vehicle to the Redcar via Whitby service. New in January 1968 it is seen here passing the Theatre Royal in St Leonard's Place, York, whilst making its way to Redcar in June 1971. The following month the Greenwood family would be on board.*

All photographs by the author.

*Four of Wallace Arnold's Plaxton-bodied AEC Reliances bask in the afternoon sunshine at Whitby's Westcliffe coach park on Saturday 3 July 1971. All were new in 1961 and formed part of the allocation of 16 coaches to Wallace Arnold's RCA contract fleet. RCA (Radio Corporation of America) built the RAF Fylingdales ballistic missile early warning system on Snod Hill in the North York Moors during the Cold War in 1963. RCA continued to maintain the station and the coaches were used to transport workers to and from their homes in Whitby.*

BELOW: *A day trip to York on Friday 9 July provided the opportunity to photograph a bus from the excellent York Pullman fleet. It is an unusual 52-seat Plaxton-bodied AEC Swift which was new in April 1970, and it is seen pulling on to the Exhibition Square stand to take up the service to Brecksfield.*

BELOW: *York's historic City Wall provided an excellent raised platform to generate a nice composition of 1965 York-West Yorkshire ECW-bodied Bristol FS6B YDX194 (EWU 875C) which was turning from Rougier Street into Station Street as it made its way to Clifton. The York-West Yorkshire Joint Committee was formed as a joint venture with York City Council back in 1932.*

ABOVE: *A visit to United's garage on Upgang Lane on Saturday 10 July found 1957 Bristol LS5G 2223 (223 CHN) waiting to take up service on the Whitby cross town route 96 between Castle Park and St Peter's Road. The front registration plate is unusually fitted above the central fog light rather than on the front bumper.*

momentum in the early 1970s there was still a sizeable proportion of Leicester's 280,000 citizens who depended entirely on public transport. Foreign holidays were still rather for the privileged few and it was, therefore, a massive logistical exercise each July

BELOW: *Visits to the UAS garage were a regular occurrence during my two week stay. On Monday 12 July I was taken by surprise when a convoy of eight coaches from the UAS fleet passed by our seafront bed-and-breakfast. What made the sight more extraordinary was that six of the coaches were former members of the Wilkinson's of Sedgefield fleet which United had purchased in February 1967. The coaches carried an ICI logo in the window and I deduced that it must have been an excursion to the seaside for retired employees of the company. I didn't have my camera with me at the time but I caught up with seven of the eight coaches later in the day parked-up inside Whitby garage.*

ABOVE: *Town route 96 was a two-bus operation and a pair of ECW-bodied Bristol LS5Gs formed the regular allocation. 2140 (WHN 140), a 45-seat bus of 1955, awaits its next shift on the service on the front forecourt of Whitby garage.*

ABOVE: *The eighth coach in the ICI convoy was parked on the garage forecourt and was 1203 (103 VHN) a 1964 ECW-bodied Bristol RELH.*

BELOW: *This classic 'United Compulsory Stop' sign was located at the foot of the 18 per cent hill on the A174 Middlesbrough road at Sandsend which is just outside Whitby. I recall that when travelling back to Whitby on a UAS Bristol MW a very young driver took over the bus at Loftus depot. He brought the bus to a stop at the top of the hill and with some difficulty and crunching eventually managed to engage first gear, as per the instruction of a similar sign, but as we started to descend the gear jumped out and we quickly picked up speed! Fortunately he was able to stop the bus through a combination of the foot and hand brake and his second attempt of engaging first gear for the descent was successful.*

to get people by coach and train to and from their UK holiday destinations.

Like many people living in the region I had gone on holidays with my parents to the East Coast resorts in the mid-1960s but my parents then became a bit more adventurous and it was bed and breakfast in the Bournemouth suburb of Boscombe in 1968, 1969 and 1970. This was a real treat for a bus enthusiast with the opportunity to sample Bournemouth's trolleybuses in July 1968 albeit it was then sad to see them all parked up, withdrawn, in Mallard Road

LEFT: *Plaxton was my favourite coachbuilder so I took the opportunity to arrange a visit to the company's works at Seamer Road in Scarborough on 13 July. I took just five photos during the visit including this one of 49-seat Bristol REMH6G 1308 (GHN 208J) which was ready to be delivered to UAS.*

depot in July 1969. The south coast resort also, of course, provided plenty to admire from the Hants & Dorset and Royal Blue fleets.

However, following this three year period when the annual journey had been south my parents chose a completely different geographic direction for July 1971 and we were heading for the North Yorkshire coastal resort of Whitby.

With access to the internet still some decades away my research in planning my activities whilst on holiday meant consulting my collection of *Buses Illustrated* magazines plus coach and rail timetables at the library.

So my adventure started at 7.25 am on Saturday 3rd July 1971 by catching the coach service from

Leicester (St. Margaret's Bus Station) to Redcar via Whitby and Saltburn which was provided by Howlett's of Quorn. Their coach for the journey north was number 31 (MNR 833F) a Bedford VAM/ Plaxton. The Howlett's timetable leaflet for the period reveals that the service operated via various Leicestershire villages and towns as the coach made its way towards the M1 motorway which it joined after completing a pick-up at East Midlands Airport at 8.20 am.

The A1 was accessed from the M1 and a 30-minute refreshment break and comfort stop was taken at the Fortes A1 service station at Barnsdale Bar at 9.25 am. Stops were scheduled at Tadcaster, York, Malton and Pickering before arrival at Whitby's Westcliffe Car Park at 12.18 pm. From Whitby the coach continued to its final destination at Redcar arriving there at 1.13 pm.

The service returned from Redcar at 2.15 pm (Saturdays from the Spring Bank Holiday Saturday to the last Saturday in September, and also on Easter Saturday). However, on Sundays in the industrial holiday fortnight, the Spring Bank Holiday Sunday and Tuesday, the late Summer Bank Holiday Sunday and Tuesday and Easter Tuesday there was an additional journey with the same 7.25 am

BELOW: *On the 15 July I took a day trip to Middlesbrough. My notes say that this photograph was taken at Middlesbrough bus station which, if that was the case, looks a little desolate with this somewhat vandalised backdrop! However, the two UAS vehicles in the red and cream dual purpose livery in contrast look very smart. They are 1121 a 1959 Bristol MW6G and 6033 a 1970 Bristol RELL6G.*

LEFT: *The real purpose of my day trip to Middlesbrough was to see if I could photograph any of the eight ex-Leicester City Transport PD2s which Teeside Municipal Transport had acquired in 1970. I was fortunate to get this rather nice shot of H146 (FJF 186).*

which was a new operator for me. A real treat during the fortnight was the arrival in Whitby of seven UAS coaches with what I believed was a large party of retired ICI workers. What made the sight particularly interesting was the fact that the convoy included a large proportion of Plaxton-bodied Leylands which were part of the fleet acquired from Wilkinson's of Sedgefield, freshly repainted in the superb olive green and cream UAS coach livery.

My brother and I decided on four transport related outings during our fortnight stay; Friday 9 July to York (fares 60p single, 70p day return and £1.00 period return), Tuesday 13 July to Scarborough – specifically to have a tour of the factory of my favourite coachbuilder, Plaxton's (fares 35p single and 60p period return) and Thursday 15 July to Middlesbrough, to hopefully see and photograph the ex-Leicester City Transport PD2s recently acquired by Teeside Municipal Transport (fares 40p single and 70p period return).

The photos on these pages give a flavour of that holiday. ∎

BELOW: *Back at the alleged Middlesbrough bus station I quickly grabbed this shot of UAS 2505 (505 FHN), a 1958 ECW 45-seat Bristol MW5G before heading to the railway station to catch the train back to Whitby.*

departure from Leicester but a later return time of 4.45 pm from Redcar. This provided a day excursion opportunity with a reasonable five hours in Whitby and over eight hours in York. The coach would eventually arrive back in Leicester at 10.35 pm.

The adult fares from Leicester to Whitby on Saturdays (with the fare for the other six days in brackets) were £6.70 (£5.35) for a period return, £4.10 (£2.95) for a day return and £3.70 (£2.60) single. Day return fares on Saturdays were clearly priced to deter customers taking up seats for those staying for a week or fortnight!

Once at Whitby my parents were quite happy for me and my elder brother to do our own bus/rail thing on certain days. So armed with my camera, a trusty Zeiss Nettar, and four rolls of 120 film, each taking 12 frames, plus my note book, I went about recording what I saw. Whitby was interesting in its own right with a large variety of day excursion traffic parking up each day at the Westcliffe coach park. This was also the home for the small fleet of old Wallace Arnold coaches which were used on the RCA contract transporting workers to nearby RAF Fylingdales which was an early warning station, in use during the cold war, to detect a potential nuclear attack!

There were also the buses and coaches of United Automobile Services, which operated out of Whitby depot, and

# WHAT COLOUR IS THE BUS TODAY, MUM?

All photographs by the author.

Two Cheshire towns have seen more change than most in their bus operators over the last half century. Cliff Beeton tells the tale.

ABOVE: *North Western Bristol RE 382 (SJA 382K) was one of the last buses delivered new to the company in 1972, with later buses from the same batch being delivered direct to successor Crosville in its green livery. 382 was repainted by Crosville into North Western colours before withdrawal in 1982 to mark ten years since the break up of North Western. It is seen at Hanley in June 1984.*

Most parts of England have seen changes to their main bus operators since the early 1970s, with the establishment and subsequent privatisation of the National Bus Company, and with it the change from many original classic liveries to the rigidly standardised NBC poppy red and leaf green schemes.

Following privatisation these would be swept away by a multitude of new liveries, some bright and brash, others more sedate, as new owners attempted to promote their own brand on the their newly-acquired businesses. The Congleton and Macclesfield areas seem to have had more changes to owners and liveries than most.

For many years the bus services in and around Macclesfield and Congleton were operated by the North Western Road Car Co, with buses in the company's red and cream livery. Services were run

BELOW: *Ex-North Western Alexander-bodied Daimler Fleetline FJA 213D, now Crosville DDG312, is seen at Biddulph Park Lane Estate on a K87 from Congleton in March 1981, shortly before the Fleetlines were replaced by new Bristol VRTs.*

from garages at Sunderland Street, Macclesfield and Walley Street, Biddulph. The garage at Biddulph, which was opened in 1960, was unusual in that it was a joint garage with Potteries Motor Traction, a fellow British Electric Traction group company. Macclesfield garage had been opened by North Western in 1939.

The South East Lancashire and North East Cheshire Passenger Transport Executive was formed in 1969 and absorbed of all the municipal operators in the Greater Manchester area. Although this did not directly affect North Western at that time, it would see the company cease to exist by 1972.

The majority of North Western's local bus services were in the Selnec area, and it was announced in 1971 that Selnec would take over all of these. The remaining services were shared between sister NBC operators Crosville and Trent.

North Western's Macclesfield and Biddulph garages thus became Crosville property from March 1972, and gradually the buses were repainted from red and cream into the light green and cream Crosville

ABOVE: *Following the sale of Crosville to Drawlane by ATL Holdings another new livery of bright green, cream and red with a smiling cartoon lynx was introduced, seen here on Bristol VRT DVL352 (WDM 352R).This livery looked set to usher in a promising new era which would ultimately prove to be short-lived as it would be the last for Crosville before the company was dismembered.*

livery. Gradually, following an NBC edict, the Crosville green and cream livery would be succeeded by NBC leaf green. The buses also gained Crosville alpha-numeric fleet numbers. Route numbers were altered, too, with Crosville letter-prefixed numbers being adopted. Macclesfield routes were allocated the prefix E whereas those in the Congleton and Biddulph area were allocated K, the same prefix as was used by Crosville at Crewe.

For a while the buses at both former North Western garages were pure North Western, albeit now green, but transfers from other Crosville depots brought unfamiliar vehicles like Bristol Lodekkas and Bristol LHs into the area.

In 1980 following NBC's Market Analysis Project, PMT announced that it was closing the jointly-owned Biddulph garage in Walley Street. This would be too large and costly for the Crosville allocation on its own, so Crosville opened a small depot at the top end of Congleton cattle market with a parking area and a Portakabin. This was classified as an outstation of Macclesfield, where all maintenance was subsequently carried out. A withdrawn ECW-bodied Bristol LH was delivered to Congleton outstation and used as a store room for consumables like oil and antifreeze and various spare parts. An old Ford fuel tanker was acquired, painted into Crosville leaf green livery and used to fuel the vehicles. In latter years the

BELOW: *During the run-up to local bus deregulation and the privatisation of the National Bus Company, Crosville started experimenting with new liveries. The first was this Brunswick green and orange with a leaping lynx, seen here on Leyland National SNG406 (KMA 406T) at the Congleton outstation ready to work a K87 to Biddulph.*

LEFT: *After a few buses were repainted into the Brunswick green and orange livery, Crosville decided to change the orange to dark cream, the end result resembling the pre-NBC Maidstone & District scheme. Bristol VRT DVL494 (WTU 494W) looks immaculate at Congleton cattle market in March 1988.*

ABOVE: *Following the division of Crosville the new C-Line operation simply added the C-Line fleetname where the Crosville fleetname had been. The new look is seen on Bristol VRT DVL389 (FTU 389T) at Congleton Fairground. C-Line kept the Crosville alpha-numeric fleet numbers but got rid of the letter prefix to the route number.*

outstation moved to the rear of the cattle market site.

Regular deliveries of standard NBC Bristol VRTs, Leyland Nationals and Leyland Leopard coaches gradually eroded the North Western heritage of the fleet. The last ex-North Western Daimler Fleetlines were withdrawn by Crosville in 1981, with the last Marshall-bodied Bristol REs following in 1983.

With the privatisation of NBC on the horizon in 1985, the rigid NBC shackles on standard bus liveries were gradually relaxed allowing Crosville to introduce a new dark green and orange livery, with a fleetname incorporating a leaping lynx. This was to be short lived as the orange was soon replaced by cream, creating a very attractive livery akin to the pre-NBC Maidstone and District scheme.

Local bus deregulation in 1986 would see other operators trying to muscle in on Crosville's traditional operating area. In Congleton local coach operator Bostocks would register competing services on the Congleton Town routes, using Leyland Leopard coaches. Crosville introduced Freight Rover Sherpa minibuses under the Mini Lynx brand to see off this challenge.

In Macclesfield another coach operator, Shearings, successfully submitted tenders for some of the services that Crosville didn't register commercially and obtained a fleet of ex-West Midlands Travel Leyland Nationals to operate them. Initially these ran in West Midlands blue and cream livery until repainted into Shearings attractive yellow, cream and orange.

Shearings would go on to purchase new Leyland Lynx and Leyland Tiger buses with Alexander (Belfast) bodywork to replace the Leyland Nationals,

resulting in a very modern fleet. Shearings latterly decided to concentrate solely on its coaching activities, with the buses being sold to a management buyout and renamed Timeline.

The privatisation of NBC got under way with the first sales in 1986, but Crosville was one of the last to be sold, passing in March 1988 to ATL Holdings (Western). ATL proprietor Tony Lavin also owned SUT in Sheffield and Yelloway in Rochdale along with bus dealership Carlton PSV. Crosville would be under ATL ownership for less than 12 months but it would be a controversial 12 months. ATL was viewed by some observers as an asset stripper, and promptly sold all the newest coaches. It also planned to close Crewe bus station and sell the site for redevelopment, closing the garage and moving the buses out to an industrial unit, but a covenant clause on the site dictated that it could only be redeveloped if it included a new bus station, so ATL quietly shelved the plans. Trouble with the traffic commissioners over vehicle maintenance was always simmering just below the surface.

ATL sold Crosville to Drawlane in February 1989, which on paper looked a much safer pair of hands. A new livery of bright green, cream and red with a smiley cartoon lynx was soon introduced; minibuses were branded as Mini Lynx with larger vehicles as Town Lynx. This looked to usher in a promising new era, but would prove to be short-lived as Drawlane would announce the dismantling of the company later that year.

This subsequently took place, with the Macclesfield and Congleton operations transferred to fellow Drawlane subsidiary The Bee Line Buzz Company,

BELOW: *The second Leyland National Greenway prototype was allocated to C-Line at Macclesfield. It was a rebuild of a former North Western and Ribble Leyland National. SNG875 (LRF 875X) is seen here when new in May 1992 at Keele University on the Sunday Staffordshire Council tendered route 53, Keele University to Baddeley Green.*

ABOVE: *Being a predominately single-deck fleet Midland Red never received any Bristol VRT double-deckers new, with most coming into the fleet when it took control of Crosville's Crewe depot. This is 1884 (WTU 484W) in the red, white and yellow livery at Congleton Fairground in 1993 working a 92 to Buglawton Estate with C-Line Midland Red fleetnames.*

which had depots at Bredbury and Stockport. Its livery was yellow, red and black. In 1990 it was announced that the Congleton and Macclesfield operations would keep the Crosville dark green and cream livery and would operate as a stand alone company, The C-Line Bus Company, from January 1991.The first and only new buses for C-Line would arrive that year in the form of six Mercedes-Benz

BELOW: *C-Line was allocated some ex-London Country South West Plaxton-bodied Leyland Tiger coaches that had been used on the Green Line network across London. ETL160 (A160 EPA) is seen here at Gawsworth in June 1993. It is working on the 38 from Crewe to Macclesfield, an interurban route for which the Tigers were ideally suited.*

811D midibuses with Carlyle 33-seat bodywork; 23 similar vehicles were delivered to the main Bee Line fleet at the same time, but in its yellow, red and black livery. Also joining the fleet in May 1992 was the second prototype Leyland National Greenway, an ex-Ribble Leyland National 2 that had come in to Drawlane ownership via North Western (a new company based in Bootle, not the original Cheshire-based business), and was rebuilt by East Lancashire Coachbuilders (also owned by Drawlane) into what was essentially a brand new bus. Other additions to the fleet were ex-Colchester Borough Transport ECW-bodied Leyland Atlanteans, and Bristol VRTs from Midland Red which had originated with Crosville at Crewe. Former London Country South West Plaxton-bodied Leyland Tiger coaches, latterly used on the Green Line network, were transferred in for the trunk 38 Macclesfield to Crewe route.

  C-Line kept the Crosville alpha-numeric fleet number system, applying it to additions to the fleet, but did away with the prefix letter on route numbers.

ABOVE: *After C-Line was absorbed into the Midland Red fleet buses started to be repainted into its red, white and yellow livery. A Macclesfield garage regular, Leyland Olympian 1952 (A152 UDM), loads in Macclesfield for Manchester in August 1993.*

C-Line was successful in winning Staffordshire County Council contracts, taking its vehicles into the Potteries on Sundays on PMT route 53 from Keele to Baddeley Green. A refreshed livery was later introduced with more cream and less green.

In 1992 Drawlane was restructured as British Bus which was by then the second largest bus group in the country.

Further reorganisation in 1993 would see the Congleton outstation closed and vehicles transferred to the Midland Red North depot at Etruria, Stoke-on-Trent, which was operated as an outstation of Crewe. The decline in livestock sales following the BSE scare had forced the closure of Congleton cattle market, which was sold for housing.

The short tenure of C-Line at Macclesfield would finish later that year when it would come under Midland Red North control. Rumours had been circulating that Macclesfield would be sold to PMT following its purchase of the Crosville Wirral and Chester operations a few years earlier, but this came to nothing. Vehicles started to be repainted into the Midland Red North yellow, red and white livery and

the vehicles were renumbered into the Midland Red North fleet number series. Some buses appeared with C-Line Midland Red fleetnames. Further livery changes would see buses painted into the original Midland Red dark red livery with gold 'Midland' fleetnames and fleet numbers. These looked smart when freshly painted but began to look tatty after a while in service. Second-hand vehicles from the main Midland Red North fleet would start to supplement the existing fleet, especially ECW-bodied Leyland Olympians replacing the ex-Colchester Atlanteans and some Bristol VRTs.

The purchase of Stevensons of Uttoxeter by British Bus in 1994 would have far-reaching consequences for Macclesfield, as it was decided to transfer its operations from Midland Red North to Stevensons' control. So once again the buses would receive a new livery, this time Stevensons yellow with black and white relief. Another renumbering exercise was implemented with the fleet being numbered into the Stevensons series. For the enthusiast this would be a very interesting era, as many of Stevensons odd-ball vehicles would end up being transferred to Macclesfield, some for just a few weeks others being permanent fixtures. Interesting arrivals included ex-Kelvin Central Alexander-bodied Metrobuses, ex-Citybus Belfast Leyland Lynxes with Alexander bodies, two Optare Spectras, Alexander-bodied Leyland Olympians purchased new by

BELOW: *For the enthusiast the Stevensons era was the most interesting as a plethora of non-standard vehicles would appear in service at Macclesfield. Parked at the back of the garage in July 1995 is Stevensons 261 (HXI 3011), a Leyland Lynx with Alexander (Belfast) bodywork which had been new to Citybus in Belfast.*

Stevensons and Q246 FVT, the Leyland Olympian B45 unregistered test-bed prototype with ECW bodywork, which Stevensons fitted out with ex-London Transport DMS seats.

So in November 1994 the former Congleton outstation operations that were now worked by Midland Red North from its depot at Etruria were moved to the former Crystal Coaches depot at Burslem, Stoke-on-Trent, and came under Stevensons control. The Stevensons livery would subsequently be modified with red relief in 1996, and would become very similar to that of Midland Red North. Ultimately the Stevensons fleet would be completely integrated and renumbered into the Midland Red North fleet.

Ex-Timeline Leyland Tiger buses with Alexander bodies were transferred into the fleet to operate the busier routes, with a batch of brand new Mercedes-Benz minibuses with Alexander Sprint bodywork for the town services.

The sale of British Bus to Cowie in 1996 would see an end to the continual merry-go-round change in colour of the Macclesfield fleet, for in 1997 Cowie would rebrand as Arriva. Whereas Drawlane and British Bus had always let their bus operating companies choose their own individual liveries, Arriva decided on a corporate livery of Cotswold stone and aquamarine that would eventually encompass the whole fleet. It would last ten years before being modified with less Cotswold stone and the addition of darker blue. This would then last almost another ten years until the revamped new pale blue scheme in 2016.

Macclesfield became part of Arriva Midlands which had various depots in the region including Burslem,

BELOW: *Following the integration of Stevensons into the Midland Red North fleet more unusual vehicles appeared at Macclesfield including ex-Timeline Leyland Tigers with Alexander (Belfast) N-type bodywork such as 1772 (F52 ENF), in the later yellow, red and white livery. It is in Congleton in 1996, working a 38 to Macclesfield.*

ABOVE: *On 5 April 2009 Arriva North West used the last former Crosville vehicle left in the fleet, ECW-bodied Leyland Olympian 3122 (C212 GTU), to work a day's duty on the 38 Crewe to Macclesfield service. Complete with the former Crosville route number K38 set on the blinds it leaves Congleton with an afternoon journey to Macclesfield.*

Crewe, Stafford, Burton upon Trent and Uttoxeter. Arriva Midlands made the decision in September 1999 to sell the Burslem depot, which operated the Congleton area services, to Matthews Motors of Leycett near Newcastle-under-Lyme which used the Handybus fleetname. The former pre-Stevensons Crystal Coaches fleetname would be reactivated by Matthews Motors for these services. Before the sale went through all vehicles in Arriva and Stevensons livery were transferred out and replaced with surplus vehicles from Shrewsbury. This saw the complete withdrawal from Congleton by Arriva, except for the trunk route 38.

Crystal Coaches unfortunately did not last too long, following maintenance problems with the traffic commissioners. This saw PMT and local independents taking over the Congleton services. PMT ran the 99 between Biddulph and Congleton

BELOW: *Few Leyland Swifts received Arriva livery, but one that did was 1131 (J31 SFA), an ex-Stevensons bus with Wright Handybus body. It is leaving the old Macclesfield bus station for Manchester in 1999.*

ABOVE: *Ladyline Coaches of Congleton used ECW-bodied Bristol LH OJD 55R in this bright orange livery for its Congleton town services. New to London Transport, it came to Ladyline after a spell with OK Motor Services of Bishop Auckland. It carries the Ladyline Local fleetname and is seen here having a break at Rode Heath in April 2006.*

for a while with vehicles in its red and yellow livery, before Bakers of Biddulph took over with buses in yellow and blue. Ladyline had a share in the Congleton town services using vehicles in a mainly cream livery that was later changed to bright orange. Interestingly Ladyline obtained some of the former C-Line Mercedes-Benz minibuses to work these services as well as an an ex-London Transport and OK Motor Services ECW-bodied Bristol LH. Bakers would latterly take over the Congleton town services with three brand new Plaxton Primo midibuses painted green and running as the Beartown Bus under a five-year council tender.

As time went by Macclesfield began to receive cascaded buses from around the Arriva fleet to gradually replace standard ex-Crosville, Midland Red and Stevensons vehicles. Ex-Caldaire Leyland Lynxes arrived for the 38 and 130, running from Macclesfield to Crewe and Manchester respectively. Then more double-deckers began to arrive, with Volvo Olympians from Maidstone & District and Arriva Wales. The now very popular Dennis Dart would make an appearance, too, with examples from many different bodybuilders including East Lancs, Plaxton, Carlyle, Duple and Wrights. These Darts would eventually go on to replace the van-derived minibuses

and ex-Stevensons Leyland Swifts in the fleet.

In 2002 Macclesfield was transferred to Arriva North West with the fleet being renumbered into the Arriva North West system at the same time. In 2004 the main Macclesfield depot at Sunderland Street was closed, having been sold for redevelopment as a doctors' surgery. The extensive depot yard had been getting smaller over the years as parts were sold off to a local car dealership. This had led to buses being parked overnight in the bus station,

BELOW: *Three new VDL DB300 double-deckers with lowheight Wright Gemini 2 bodywork were delivered to Macclesfield in 2011 for the trunk route 38 to Crewe. These were upgraded to Sapphire standard in April 2015.*

where gates were fitted across the main entrance. A new smaller bus station was opened nearer the town centre in April 2004. The fleet was then allocated to an outstation at Gaw End Lane, Lyme Green, on the outskirts of the town. Macclesfield would from now on be merely an outstation of Winsford, which had itself been established following the closure of the depot at Crewe. All maintenance would now be carried out at Winsford.

On 5 April 2009 the last former Crosville vehicle in the Arriva North West fleet, ECW-bodied Leyland Olympian 3122 (C212 GTU), formerly EOG 212, was allocated to Macclesfield for the day to operate on the 38 Macclesfield to Crewe service, with the number blinds showing K38, its former Crosville route number.

During the Arriva era Macclesfield was the recipient of various batches of new buses, with Alexander Dennis Mini Pointer Darts arriving for the town services in 2000. These were replaced by a fleet of Optare Solo SRs branded as The Silk Link in 2012. Three brand-new VDL DB300 double deckers with Wright Eclipse Gemini lowheight bodywork arrived at the end of 2011 for trunk route 38; these were the first new double-deckers at Macclesfield since ECW-bodied Leyland Olympians in 1984. They were very popular on the route and in 2014 it was decided to refurbish them to the premium Sapphire specification with a stylish new livery, e-leather seats and phone charging points. Rear destination equipment was fitted at the same time. The refurbished buses were launched in April 2015. Macclesfield gained work on the 130 service to Manchester from Manchester depot in 2016, acquiring a fleet of Wright Solar-bodied VDL SB200s to operate it. These were subsequently refurbished to Sapphire standard the same as the double-deckers, and did occasionally appear on the 38, too.

GHA Coaches of Ruabon had first arrived in the area in 2009 when its Vale of Llangollen subsidiary started operating school contracts from an outstation in Heapy Street, this being replaced by a more suitable one in Moss Lane in 2015. GHA would subsequently win tenders for local bus services, starting with the evening service on the 130 in January 2013. It would go on to work the 9 to Moss Rose, 10 to Bollington and evening journeys on the

ABOVE: *Bakerbus launched the Beartown Bus network in Congleton in August 2007 using three brand new Plaxton Primo midibuses in a green livery to operate the four routes. DX07 WEH is at Congleton Fairground in April 2011.*

trunk 38. In Congleton it took the town services and the 42, Congleton to Crewe. In 2014 brand-new ADL Enviro200 buses were delivered for the 42, branded as Gold Service in a smart red, gold and cream livery with leather seats and charging points for mobile phones. In 2015 the Congleton town services received two brand new Enviro200s in a bright green livery for the revamped Beartown Bus network.

The sudden collapse of GHA Coaches in July 2016 saw Arriva gain route 87, Macclesfield to Congleton via Buglawton and Lyme Green, on a temporary tender using Optare Solo SR models. Arriva had only been serving Congleton on the trunk route 38 since the sale of the Burslem depot in 1999. In Macclesfield Arriva regained the evening services on the 38, the 9 and the 10 on temporary and then permanent contracts with Cheshire East Council. The Beartown network would pass to D&G Bus on a temporary contract along with the 42. Hollinshead Coaches won the permanent contract for the Beartown Network with two brand new Enviro200s; these are still running in a white pending a new Beartown Bus livery decision by Cheshire East Council.

In 2017 the new Arriva livery of a pale blue was launched, with buses starting to be repainted again. The first brand-new buses delivered in the new livery were Mercedes-Benz Sprinters for the Macclesfield town services, which replaced the five-year-old Solos, promising to usher in a new era for the town services that over the years have gone from large vehicles to minibuses, then back to larger vehicles only to revert back again to smaller ones. ∎

# LONDON'S COLOURFUL BUSES

ABOVE: *The reorganisation of London Buses in 1989 saw the creation of new companies, such as East London, owner of this Leyland Titan. But the buses were still, generally, red.*

LEFT: *The way things were. At the start of the 1980s London's buses were red, and Routemasters were still a common sight.*

There was a revolution in London in the late 1980s, when a new tendering regime saw multi-coloured buses challenge the supremacy of the traditional red livery. **Stewart J Brown** looks at the rise of independent operators in the first five years of tendered operation.

London's buses are red. Somewhere in the depths of the LT Museum archives there's probably a tablet of stone inscribed with these very words. But that changed in the mid 1980s - in July 1985, to be exact - and for much of the following 15 years or so London bus passengers were faced not only with red buses, but buses featuring combinations of green, blue, grey, yellow, brown, purple, orange and white, too.

It was the rainbow era, the result of route tendering introduced under the 1984 London Regional Transport Act. Before the Act came into force London Transport operated the vast majority of the capital's buses. Under the Act responsibility for planning the route network and the level of service lay with London Regional Transport, while the operational fleet of almost 5,200 buses was taken over on 1 April

1985 by a new LRT subsidiary, London Buses Ltd. To inject a measure of the competition so beloved by Margaret Thatcher's Conservative government, and to reduce costs, LRT was required to invite operators to tender for individual routes, and later for local route networks. This process got under way at the end of 1984 with the announcement that 13 suburban routes were being put out to tender.

For the early tenders LRT chose services on the outskirts of London which required relatively small numbers of vehicles. This was intended to make the routes more attractive to smaller operators, and also acknowledged the difficulty any newcomers would face in finding garage space for buses close to central London.

The contracts were awarded for up to five years and

*National Bus Company subsidiaries around London secured a number of contracts from LRT. Among the first was Eastern National, with Bedford midibuses in North London. The route number should read W9.*

were gross cost contracts, where the operator quoted on the basis that LRT retained the revenue collected on the routes. So, as long as they had calculated their costs correctly, there was no revenue-related financial risk to the operators, another feature which made tendering attractive to small businesses.

Some well-known coach operators were quick to see potential benefits in bidding for LRT contracts, and in the late 1980s Grey-Green, Cityrama, Len Wright, Scancoaches and Pan Atlas would appear as bus operators. Although the profit margins may have been low, LRT contracts provided a guaranteed cash flow, which is something that could not be said of most coach operations where, even in London with its year-round tourism, there was still a measure of seasonality.

Twelve tenders were awarded by LRT in 1985, with six routes being retained by London Buses and six going to four new operators, two independents and two National Bus Company subsidiaries.

NBC subsidiary Eastern National took over two services. On the W9, Enfield to Muswell Hill, red London Buses' BL-class Bristol LHs were replaced by four-year-old green and cream Bedford YMQ-S midibuses with Wadham Stringer Vanguard bodies. These unusual Bedfords had 33 high-backed seats, bringing a rare touch of luxury to a local London bus service.

On the 193, Romford to Hornchurch, Eastern National briefly used standard NBC ECW-bodied Bristol VRTs, but after a few weeks the service was converted to minibus operation as the Hornchurch

Hoppa – the first of many Hoppa-branded routes which would bounce around the LRT area.

The other NBC subsidiary was London Country Bus Services, which also won two routes. For the 313, Potters Bar to Chingford, it initially used ECW-bodied Leyland Olympians. The P4, Brixton to Lewisham, was covered by four Leyland Nationals based at the Catford garage of National Travel London and carried National London fleetnames.

The two independents which figured in the first round of tender awards were Len Wright Travel and Crystals of Orpington. Len Wright Travel in the 1980s was best known for exotic coaches used to carry pop groups. It won the 81, Hounslow to Slough, and for this bought nine 10-year-old London

BELOW: *In the early days of tendering a few small operators won contracts for routes in Outer London. These included Metrobus of Orpington, which would grow to become a major player in south-east London. The bus is a Bedford YMT with Wadham Stringer body.*

ABOVE: *Not all of the operators who won tenders were successful. Sampsons of Cheshunt, owner of this ex-London Fleetline in service in Enfield, only operated on LRT routes for two years.*

ABOVE: *Scancoaches was the first independent to win a tender using new buses, Jonckheere-bodied Scanias. It operated the 283 in West London from 1986 to 1989.*

ABOVE: *It might look like an ex-London DMS-type Fleetline, but this Grey-Green EastenderBus originated with the South Yorkshire PTE. It was operated by Grey-Green subsidiary Dix Luxury Coaches of Dagenham.*

Transport Fleetlines, which operated under the London Buslines name in a yellow and brown livery derived from that used on the company's coaches. Len Wright was not alone in winning LRT business using Fleetlines which had been discarded by LT as unsuitable for operation in the capital. Was anyone at LT embarrassed that small operators with relatively limited resources could apparently make these buses work when LT with its massive workshops couldn't? Probably not.

Crystals of Orpington took over the 146, Bromley North to Downe. For a few months this was operated using existing vehicles in the Crystals fleet, but at the start of 1986 the company took delivery of a pair of unusual Leyland Cubs with 33-seat Lex Maxeta bodies. These did not have route number blinds; the route number was painted on the front dome.

To reassure passengers that all these colourful vehicles really were London buses, the new contractors' buses displayed a sticker on the front with the LRT roundel alongside the words *London Regional Transport Service*. The use by operators of their own liveries was not an issue in the mid 1980s. Clear identification of the company running each service introduced a measure of operator accountability, which it was hoped would help raise standards. There was also a suggestion that Margaret Thatcher, a staunch proponent of private enterprise, insisted that private companies use their own liveries rather than paint their buses red. That tale may be apocryphal; it's hard to imagine the Iron Lady concerning herself about such mundane things as the colours of the buses on suburban London services.

To try and beat the new incoming operators at their own game, London Buses created two subsidiaries in 1986 in which staff were employed on lower wage rates and with different working agreements from the main business. These were Stanwell Buses in West London and Orpington Buses in the south-east, and both were successful in winning LRT contracts which started in the summer of 1986.

Stanwell Buses, which traded as Westlink, took over the operation of three services in the Hounslow area. It was a low-cost unit and it looked it. Stanwell Buses had a fleet of 28 Leyland Nationals - typically around 10 years old - which had been transferred from London Buses and tarted up with the addition of white and turquoise relief along the waist and Westlink names on the front.

On the other hand Orpington Buses was a classy-looking operation set up with 29 new minibuses in an attractive maroon and grey livery and branded as Roundabout. The buses were 24 Iveco 49.10s with Robin Hood City Nippy bodies, and five stylish Optare CityPacers built on MAN-VW LT55 chassis which, as time would show, were not quite up to the job. But they looked good, and they were the first of this new type to enter service.

NBC's London Country and Eastern National expanded in London in 1986.

London Country's operations ringed the capital and it gained services in a number of areas. These included not only parts of outer London such as Orpington and Watford, but a route closer to the heart of the capital with the 268 in Hampstead. If there was any doubt that the world was changing, it was surely erased by the operation of a London bus route by a state-owned company, running from a base at a motorway service area, Scratchwood on the M1. The 268 – the Hampstead Hoppa - was operated by new Mercedes-Benz L608 van conversions which after a few months were replaced by Dodge S56s with Reeve Burgess bodies.

For those routes needing full-size buses, London Country bought second-hand Atlanteans. A dozen came from sister NBC operators Southdown and Brighton & Hove, but of more interest were 31 from the Strathclyde PTE, which had Alexander bodies with panoramic windows. London Country's expansion in 1986 included routes right round the capital in Watford, South Mimms, Orpington, Tooting, Croydon and Epsom.

With 1,200 vehicles London Country was NBC's biggest subsidiary and in preparation for privatisation – another Conservative Big Idea -  it was divided into four separate companies in September 1986 with geographical identities – London Country South West, South East, North East and North West, with each taking over the LRT contracts in their areas.

Eastern National's new services in 1986 were all on the eastern and north-eastern edges of London and the company opened a new 32-vehicle base in Walthamstow. Eastern National added Citybus names to those vehicles, mainly Bristol VRTs, which it was running on LRT services. The use of Bristol VRTs on LRT contracts was unusual, and Eastern National was the only company to run them in significant numbers.

Metrobus of Orpington had been running buses on the edge of London for some years and won its first LRT contracts in 1986. In its choice of vehicles it followed in the footsteps of London Buslines, buying 13 redundant LT Fleetlines from Ensign Bus, the dealer which had shrewdly cornered the market in LT's unwanted DMs and DMSs. These increased the Metrobus fleet to 24 vehicles. Other tender wins saw Metrobus buying three new Bedford YMTs with

ABOVE: *The EastenderBus name was not perpetuated and subsequent acquisitions for LRT services carried the Grey-Green name, oddly inappropriate on a white, orange and brown bus such as this Leyland Lynx.*

ABOVE: *Harrow Buses operated smart new MCW Metrobuses and Metroriders, but its fleet also included 26 ex-West Midlands Ailsas. There are no obvious signs that Harrow Buses was part of London Buses.*

ABOVE: *When route tendering got under way, London Buses actually bought back 14 of the Fleetlines which it had been so eager to discard just a few years earlier. This bus was purchased from Clydeside Scottish. Bexleybus was a London Buses subsidiary, but looked like an independent.*

LEFT: *Late deliveries of new buses was a common problem facing LRT contractors. Boro'line's Optare-bodied Leyland Olympians were slow to arrive and the company had to hire buses such as the Hull Atlantean on the right to cover its LRT commitments.*

Scanbus fleetnames were carried, and the Belgian-produced destination blinds offered 'Schepherds Bush' as one of the places served. Scanbus operated the service for three years.

Grey-Green was one of the best-known names in London coaching, and had its headquarters in Stamford Hill. It had since 1981 been in the ownership of the Cowie Group. In 1987 the company took on its first LRT contract, in East London, and put it under the control of its Dagenham-based subsidiary, Dix. For this it bought ten South Yorkshire PTE Fleetlines, all with DMS-style MCW bodies making them look more or less at home in the capital except, of course, that they weren't red. The livery adopted was white, orange and brown, and the vehicles carried EastenderBus fleetnames, rather than Grey-Green or Dix. The EastenderBus name was not used on any other vehicles.

In 1987 Grey-Green took on three more services in north-east London, for which it bought a dozen former Greater Manchester Fleetlines, six new Leyland Lynxes and six East Lancs-bodied Scania N112 double-deckers. All were in the same white, orange and brown livery as used on the Dix Fleetlines, but with Grey-Green fleetnames, although neither grey nor green paint was used on the vehicles.

One of the original independent operators, London Buslines, expanded in 1987 using ex-Greater Manchester Fleetlines. At the same time it purchased six new Leyland Lynxes to replace the ex-London Fleetlines which the company had been using on its first tendered service and which were proving increasingly unreliable.

Other buyers of redundant Greater Manchester buses in 1987 included London Country South West which needed them for new LRT contracts, with some being pressed into services in Manchester brown, orange and white.

Thus far operators had been supplying their own vehicles, usually second-hand double-deckers. But in 1987 when London Country North West won two contracts for Hoppa minibus services one, the Holloway Hoppa, used new LCNW-owned Iveco 49.10s, but the other, the C2 Camden Hoppa, was

automatic gearboxes and Wadham Stringer Vanguard bodies, followed in 1987 by 11 second-hand Leyland Olympians with Roe bodies - just four and five years old – acquired from the West Yorkshire PTE.

As well as being a dealer, Ensign Bus appeared as a bus operator on LRT services in 1986, winning a route in Dagenham which was not far from the company's Purfleet base. With its experience in handling the sale of ex-London Fleetlines, it goes without saying that these are what appeared on its LRT service, in a smart blue and silver livery. A second contract win in 1987 took Ensign's LRT Fleetline fleet to 18 vehicles.

Following Len Wright's lead, more coach operators were bidding successfully for LRT contracts. Cityrama appeared in south London in 1986, using ex-London Fleetlines painted dark blue and white. Cityrama won a second South London route in 1987, and for this added more Fleetlines to its fleet including 11 with unusual ECW highbridge bodies which came from the South Yorkshire PTE. In the north, Sampson's of Cheshunt took over a service in Enfield, operating it with seven ex-London Fleetlines in an unusual blue and purple livery.

Perhaps the most interesting of the new operators in 1986 was Scancoaches, a well-respected business whose name reflected the Scandinavian origins of its owners. Scancoaches took on a service in west London in May, and the company had the distinction of being the first independent to win an LRT tender on the basis of operating new rather than second-hand buses. They were unusual buses too: five 12m-long Scania K92s with Jonckheere Trans-City bodies. They were the first maximum-length buses to run a regular service in London, and had the first examples of Jonckheere bus bodywork in Britain.

run using 25 Optare CityPacers owned by LRT. The Holloway Hoppas were green; the Camden Hoppas were in London red. Both routes were operated for just 14 months because LCNW lost the use of a BRS depot in Muswell Hill where it garaged the vehicles. The contracts were then re-allocated to London Buses.

Things were not going too well at London Country North East. In late January and early February 1988 a 10-day strike over revised conditions of employment saw two other operators stepping in to cover the company's three LRT contracts. Grey-Green provided Duple-bodied Leyland Leopard coaches for two services, while Borehamwood Travel Services operated the third, also with Leopard coaches. This short-term arrangement continued when the strike ended, as LCNE advised LRT that it did not have enough staff to cover its contracts.

Six-month contracts for the three routes were then awarded to Grey-Green and BTS, followed by permanent contracts later in the year. For its two routes Grey-Green acquired ten South Yorkshire Metrobuses, some of which were initially used in South Yorkshire colours. BTS bought Leyland Nationals from West Yorkshire Road Car; most were in NBC poppy red livery, which BTS adopted as its fleet colour. The Nationals were replaced by six new Alexander-bodied Scania N113 double-deckers in 1989.

There was a new look for London Country South West in the spring of 1987, when the business was renamed the Kentish Bus & Coach Co with a striking new cream and maroon livery replacing the unimaginative NBC green.

Not all of the colour in London came from new operators. London Buses' Orpington Buses fleet was maroon and grey. And London Buses won two major networks in the winter of 1987-88 in Harrow and Bexley. Harrow Buses adopted cream and red for its fleet, which included new MCW Metrobus IIs and Metroriders; the latter were Harrow Hoppas. Late delivery of the Metrobuses saw the Harrow Buses operation being launched with a rag-tag collection of ex-Greater Manchester Fleetlines. Late deliveries of new vehicles would become a regular occurrence, with hired vehicles briefly adding colour but subtracting quality on some LRT services.

The Bexleybus fleet was cream and

blue, and included new Northern Counties-bodied Leyland Olympians and DMS Fleetlines purchased from Clydeside Scottish, which were presumably supplied with a generous portion of humble pie as now even a London Buses subsidiary was admitting it could make these much-maligned buses work.

Bexleybus ran the bulk of the Bexley network with a fleet of 107 vehicles, with the remaining routes being operated by local-authority-owned Maidstone Borough Transport, which traded as Boro'line Maidstone. Boro'line took on four routes for which it ordered 14 Leyland Olympians with Optare bodies. As in Harrow, late deliveries affected Boro'line, and it started its LRT operations with 14 Roe-bodied Atlanteans hired from Kingston-upon-Hull City Transport. Ultimately Boro'line took 11 of the Optare Olympians and cancelled three, replacing them with two stock Alexander-bodied Scanias and a Volvo Citybus demonstrator.

Bexleybus suffered from a shortage of drivers which affected service reliability, and towards the

BELOW: *Boro'line was an attractive re-branding of what had been Maidstone Borough Transport. This Alexander-bodied Ailsa had been new to Tayside Transport.*

BELOW: *The first LRT contract won by Pan Atlas in 1988 was for a service in West London between Ealing Broadway and Brent Cross for which it bought eight new Leyland Lynxes.*

ABOVE: *Kentish Bus, formerly London Country South East, established a strong presence in London, as illustrated by two Leyland Olympians in The Strand. Kentish Bus was owned by Proudmutual of Newcastle, which also owned Northumbria Motor Services.*

end of 1988 two of its routes were transferred to Boro'line. This brought further variety, with the purchase by Boro'line of eight Alexander-bodied Ailsas from Tayside Transport.

In November 1988 Boro'line reached central London when it took on the service running from Greenwich to Euston. Here, as in Bexley at the start of the year, its new buses did not arrive in time, and the service was introduced using eight Leyland Atlanteans hired from Ipswich Borough Transport and eight Daimler Fleetlines from Nottingham City Transport, both of which were able to supply two-door vehicles, a prerequisite for operation in central London. Coincidentally, both fleets' buses were green, which created some semblance of a unified service. The new buses for the route, 14 Volvo Citybuses with Alexander bodies, arrived in the early months of 1989. Boro'line also bought 12 Leyland Lynxes in 1989 for a new route in Lewisham.

LEFT: *The first independent operator to run Dennis Darts in London was R&I Buses, which took 14 with Carlyle bodies in 1990. This is an additional bus, a former Carlyle demonstrator, in Belsize Park.*

Another new name marked the continuing interest by London coach operators in running buses. Pan Atlas, trading as Atlas Bus, took over a service in Ealing on 30 July 1988 with eight new Leyland Lynxes replacing London Buses' Nationals. The precise date is of note, because at this time the prefix letter on new vehicle registrations changed annually on 1 August - which meant that Pan Atlas's new Lynxes carried E-prefix numbers rather than the new F prefix which came into use 48 hours later. One can imagine the staff in the vehicle licensing office, battling with the huge peak in workload which accompanied the annual rush for new cars with new registrations, staring with incredulity at someone actually wanting to register new vehicles in the last two days of the old prefix. Atlas Bus added double-deckers to its fleet in 1989 with nine Leyland Olympians with Northern Counties bodies for a new contract in the Edgware area.

Both Grey-Green and Ensign Bus made significant advances in 1988. Ensign Bus took on two more routes in September which meant further fleet expansion This included 16 new MCW Metrobus IIs, Ensign's first new vehicles for LRT contracts. More former London DMS-type Fleetlines were added to the fleet too, plus four former Southampton City Transport Nationals for a service passing under a low bridge at Cranham.

A significant but short-lived new operator appeared on LRT services in the Romford area in 1988. Former NBC subsidiary East Midland Motor Services had been privatised in a management buy-out in February 1988. Under NBC ownership it had established a small commercial operation in the Brentwood area in 1986, trading as Frontrunner in a two-tone green and cream livery. This provided the springboard for expansion, and Frontrunner Buses South East was formed as an East Midland subsidiary to run two LRT services with a fleet of 30 ex-Greater Manchester Atlanteans. Stagecoach bought East Midland in April 1989 and promptly sold Frontrunner South East to Ensign Bus. Stagecoach kept the Atlanteans and Ensign used a variety of types, including eight new Alexander-bodied Olympians.

Grey-Green was the first independent to win a tender in the heart of London when it was awarded the high-profile 24 running from Pimlico to Hampstead Heath, a route which ran through

Parliament Square, Whitehall and Trafalgar Square. For this it bought 30 new Alexander-bodied Volvo Citybuses at a cost of £2.5million, or around £83,000 per vehicle. Grey-Green started running the service on 5 November 1988.

A distinctive new livery was introduced on the Citybuses using, appropriately, grey and green relieved by an orange band which reflected the Orange Luxury business, which had been part of the Ewer Group, one-time owners of Grey-Green. The orange also lightened what might otherwise have been a rather unexciting combination of colours. The livery was designed by Best Impressions and it was also applied to existing buses in the Grey-Green fleet as they became due for repaint.

For private sector operators on LRT contracts the story wasn't always one of continuing expansion. Sampson's disappeared from LRT operation in July 1988, when the contract for its only route was terminated following complaints about unreliability. London Buses took over, initially on a short-term contract which was later made permanent. Cityrama gave up one of its two LRT contracts at the end of 1988, followed by the second in 1989 bringing an end to its bus operations after three years.

Meanwhile the National Bus Company was being privatised, which meant new owners for the four London Country companies in the early months of 1988. LCNW was bought by its management in January, followed by LCSW which was taken over by Drawlane in February. Next, in March, was Kentish Bus, formerly LCSE, which was purchased by Proudmutual (owner of Northumbria Motor Services), and finally in April LCNE (which had no LRT contracts at this time) was bought by the Yorkshire-based AJS Group. In January 1989 LCNE was split in two, with County Bus & Coach serving the eastern area between Grays and Hoddesdon, and Sovereign Bus & Coach taking over the western area around Stevenage and Welwyn Garden City.

A noteworthy 1988 tender win for the newly-privatised Kentish Bus was the Surrey Quays Hoppa, which linked Surrey Docks on the south of the Thames with the Isle of Dogs on the north, reintroducing a regular bus service through the Rotherhithe Tunnel after a 20-year gap. The service was operated by MCW Metroriders.

Expansion continued at London Buslines, which took delivery of its first new double-deckers, 11 Alexander-bodied Leyland Olympians, in 1989, and then followed these in 1990 with 14 more Olympians, but with Northern Counties bodies.

| LRT tendering: Independent operators up to 1990 | |
|---|---|
| Len Wright | 1985- |
| Eastern National | 1985-90 |
| Cityrama | 1986-89 |
| Crystals | 1986- |
| Ensign Bus | 1986-90 |
| LCNE | 1986-88 |
| LCNW | 1986-90 |
| LCSE/Kentish Bus | 1986- |
| LCSW/London & Country | 1986- |
| Metrobus | 1986- |
| Sampson's | 1986-88 |
| Scancoaches | 1986-89 |
| Grey-Green | 1987- |
| Borehamwood Travel | 1988- |
| Boro'line | 1988- |
| Frontrunner | 1988-89 |
| Pan Atlas | 1988- |
| R&I | 1989- |
| Armchair | 1990- |
| County | 1990- |
| Luton & District | 1990 |
| Sovereign | 1990- |
| Thamesway | 1990- |

The 1990 Olympians were the first new buses in an improved Best Impressions-designed livery which added orange and brown relief to the base yellow, along with a new style of fleetname.

London Buslines also introduced its first minibuses to LRT operations in 1989 when it won the contract for the new C4 Fulham Hoppa. It initially used four Mercedes 609D van conversions transferred from the associated Bee Line fleet in Berkshire. In 1990 these were replaced by four new 709Ds with coachbuilt Reeve Burgess Beaver bodies.

LCSW adopted a new look in 1989, with a stylish two-tone green livery - another Best Impressions creation - and a new fleetname, London & Country. A band of red relief signified the link between the company's original green-liveried outer London operations and its growing presence in traditional red bus territory. For LRT operation in 1989 it bought 38 Volvo Citybuses, followed at the start of

BELOW: *BTS – Borehamwood Travel Services – won its first LRT tender in 1988 and gradually expanded as it secured new contracts in north-west London. This is a Northern Counties-bodied Leyland Olympian heading east on College Road, Harrow; the road is now one-way, in the opposite direction.*

1990 by six Leyland Lynxes. These were all used to replace older vehicles on existing contracts.

Another part of the former London Country business, LCNW, also bought new buses, 15 Leyland-bodied Olympians, to replace ageing Atlanteans. These were the first buses to be delivered in the company's new green and grey colour scheme.

R&I was another coach operator attracted by the opportunities opened up by London tendering. and in 1989 it won three contracts for which it bought ten Iveco 49.10s with Robin Hood bodies. High passenger loadings on one service saw the Ivecos being replaced by four unusual second-hand 37-seat Lex-bodied Bedfords, which had been new in 1982 to NBC subsidiary South Wales Transport.

By this time there were 16 private sector operators running bus services in London, and LRT claimed that around 25 per cent of services had been put out to tender, involving 1,500 buses, and that two-thirds of the tenders had been won by London Buses. In 1989 there was a major restructuring of London Buses with the creation of 11 operating companies. This was a prelude to privatisation, which took place in 1994-95.

Harry Blundred's name was never far from the headlines in the late 1980s. Blundred was a former NBC manager (at Devon General) and a proponent of high-frequency minibus operations. In March 1989 he launched Docklands Transit. Its target was to operate 100 minibuses on seven services in and around the rapidly-developing Docklands area, and by the end of the year it had gone a fair way towards achieving this, with 70 Mellor-bodied Ford Transits

buzzing around East London and through the Blackwall Tunnel to Greenwich and Lewisham.

The services were authorised by Road Service Licences granted by the Metropolitan Traffic Commissioner, in the absence of LRT's willingness to let them operate by agreement. LRT did not oppose the licence application but the three London boroughs to be served did, in part because LRT Travelcards would not be valid on the routes. In the spring of 1990 LRT allowed two routes which did not compete with established bus services to be part of the Travelcard scheme.

Blundred had an eye to the future, and to the promised deregulation of London's bus services which was still on the government's agenda. But the government was clearly getting cold feet, and in November 1990 Docklands Transit came to a sudden halt, closing down with less than two weeks' notice. One of the problems had been that because most of the services were not included in LRT's Travelcard scheme, Travelcard holders would wait for an LRT-funded bus on common sections of route rather than pay to ride on Docklands Transit.

In October 1990 LCNW was sold by its management to Luton & District Transport. Luton & District retained LCNW's green and grey livery, and added local identities. Vehicles on LRT services were given Watfordwide names, later changed to Watford Bus.

In 1990 Grey-Green and R&I expanded, each winning two routes at London Buses' expense R&I had in the main been operating Iveco minibuses, but the new contracts required bigger buses and R&I became the first independent operator of Dennis Darts in London, taking 14 with Carlyle bodies.

One of the routes which Grey-Green took over was to be operated by single-deckers and these appeared as Volvo B10Ms with 41-seat East Lancs EL2000 bodies. They were 10.3m long and had a short rear overhang to minimise accident damage caused by the outswing of the rear when turning. The B10M chassis provided a high degree of commonality with the Citybuses in the Grey-Green fleet. More double-deck Volvos were purchased, too, partly to replace older buses and partly for a new contract which took Grey-Green into south London, operating from Hampstead Heath to the Elephant & Castle.

Kentish Bus expanded significantly at the start of 1990, and added 43 two-door Northern Counties-bodied Leyland Olympians to its fleet to cover the three routes which it won from London Buses subsidiary London Forest and which took it into the heart of London, with one of the routes operating to Piccadilly Circus. The new buses cost £4million

(£93,000 each) and followed 13 similar single-door buses in 1989 which had replaced former Strathclyde Atlanteans. They brought to 80 the number of vehicles which Kentish Bus was operating on LRT contracts.

Harrow Buses lost most of its routes when they were re-tendered. A new AJS company, Sovereign Buses (Harrow), was responsible for operating much of the Harrow area network from the end of 1990, and for this it purchased 27 Mercedes-Benz with Reeve Burgess Beaver bodies. Other new contracts in the Harrow area were won by BTS Coaches, which bought 14 Northern Counties-bodied Olympians, and LCNW, with seven Workington-bodied Leyland Olympians and seven Carlyle-bodied Darts which were the first of a new, longer, 9.8m model.

The other new-look London Buses subsidiary, Bexleybus, also fared badly on re-tendering, losing work for 100 buses out of a fleet of 107. Most of the contracts went to another London Buses business, London Central (but were actually taken on by Selkent), but three routes were won by Kentish Bus, and one each by Boro'line and a new operator on LRT services, Transcity. Transcity initially used unusual Talbot Pullman six-wheel minibuses.

County Bus & Coach, part of AJS, expanded in 1990 and ordered 22 new buses for its first LRT contracts. These were eight Leyland Lynxes and 14 long-wheelbase Leyland Olympians with Northern Counties bodies.

In November 1990 Drawlane subsidiary London & Country took over two routes from London Central, the 78 and 176, one of which brought green buses to Trafalgar Square and Oxford Circus. It ordered 36 Volvo Citybuses with East Lancs bodies, but the now familiar delivery delays on new buses meant that it had to hire 24 Leyland Atlanteans from South Yorkshire Transport. These were of dual-door layout and were therefore ideal short-term hires, although the sound of an AN68 Atlantean and the sight of buses lettered Sheffield Mainline did seem surreal in Oxford Circus. Four of the SYT Atlanteans were also borrowed by BTS for a short period to cover the late arrival of its new Leyland Olympians.

Respected coach operator Armchair Passenger Transport of Brentford won two tenders in 1990. The first started in June with 12 dealer stock Leyland Olympians with lowheight Alexander R-type bodies. The second was due to start in September, but Armchair was unable to secure delivery of suitable buses in time and London & Country stepped in, using Atlanteans and Olympians on a short-term contract until January 1991 when Armchair took over with 17 Leyland-bodied Olympians.

Eastern National, which had been privatised in a management buy-out from NBC at the end of 1986, was bought by Badgerline in April 1990. In July the company was split in two, with operations in London and south Essex being taken over by a new company, Thamesway. All of Eastern National's LRT services - requiring around 90 buses - passed to Thamesway which adopted a new livery of yellow and dark maroon, later changed to the unlikely combination of yellow and purple. Thamesway's first new buses were four Leyland-bodied Olympians, purchased from the stock of Leyland dealer Arlington. These replaced some of the Bristol VRTs in Enfield.

In the space of just five years, London's buses had changed. Red was on the wane. Colour ruled. Or so, at least, it seemed. And while double-deckers still dominated London's streets there were fewer of them, with a new focus on small buses. In 1985 double-deckers made up 90 per cent of the fleet; by 1990 that figure was nearer 75 per cent.

It was a tumultuous time … and it didn't last. Gradually the small operators were squeezed out. The London Buses subsidiaries were privatised. The consolidation of the bus industry in to big groups saw British Bus, Cowie, First, Go-Ahead and Stagecoach establish a strong presence in London. Some big names – notably Connex and National Express – came and went.

And eventually, on the outside at least, it looked as if the old order was back. All London buses were once again red. As they should be. ■

*Luton & District bought London Country North East in 1990, initially retaining the company's green and grey livery. This is a Carlyle-bodied Dennis Dart in Watford. The prominent destination display was a response by Carlyle to criticism of the original design, where the destination was behind the windscreen, as shown on the R&I bus on page 64.*

# HERE TODAY, GONE TOMORROW?

Some well-known operators have vanished during the last ten years.
**Mark Bailey** illustrates a selection.

ABOVE: *McKindless was based at Newmains in Lanarkshire. Formed in 1987 the company grew to operate services across a large part of Strathclyde, including Glasgow, Motherwell, Hamilton and East Kilbride. At its peak the fleet numbered in excess of 200 vehicles, many of which were double-deckers. Pictured in Lanark in June 2003 on service 41 from Hamilton is WIL 9216, one of several rare Dennis Lance SLFs with dual-door Berkhof 2000 bodywork previously operated by Menzies at Heathrow Airport. McKindless ceased trading suddenly in February 2010.*

The Greek philosopher Heraclitus is noted for his assertion that the only constant is change. Change happens all the time – in the workplace, in politics, in sport, in the media – and on the High Street where businesses seem to come and go all too frequently. Famous names and brands disappear whilst new ones emerge and strive to gain a foothold with consumers.

Bus companies – ranging from well-established family firms to relatively new upstarts – continue to disappear for a variety of reasons. Acquisition, retirement, loss of contracts, reduced subsidies, increasing bureaucracy and red tape, unpaid debts, cash flow problems, aggressive competition, arson attacks and falling foul of the traffic commissioner have all been contributory factors in recent years. The following photographs are a reminder of some of the operators that have vanished from the scene during the last ten years. ■

LEFT: *East Sussex-based Coastal Coaches won its first contract in 1990 and latterly operated tendered services radiating from Hastings to Rye, Northiam and Tenterden with a smart modern fleet of around ten single-deckers. Seen loading in Rye in October 2009 is Alexander Dennis Dart Enviro200 125 (GX07 AVO) working service 344 from Hastings to Northiam. Following the loss of the network to Stagecoach South East at the end of July 2011 the owner decided to retire.*

ABOVE: *Norfolk Green started in 1996 and developed an extensive network of services across Norfolk and into Cambridgeshire and Lincolnshire, in the process winning awards for the quality of its operations. In 2011 it consolidated its foothold in King's Lynn when First East of England withdrew, and the fleet size grew to around 75, a quarter of which were double-deckers. A type operated for many years was the Plaxton Beaver-bodied Mercedes-Benz Vario O814, illustrated by 413 (S313 DLG) in King's Lynn bus station in February 2008. Retirement of the owner prompted the sale to Stagecoach in December 2013, which retained Norfolk Green's strong identity and livery until mid-2015 when integration into the main business commenced.*

ABOVE: *Premiere Travel of Nottingham started in 2002 and built up a network of routes stretching out to Derby, Loughborough, Newark and Mansfield, incurring retaliation from incumbent operator Trent Barton on some corridors. Fleet strength reached around 90 vehicles, mostly single-deckers. An exception was 4618 (T818 RFG), one of four East Lancs-bodied Dennis Tridents acquired from Brighton & Hove, seen in March 2012 in Hucknall on the Red 8 service to Nottingham. In January 2013 the business went into administration and subsequently closed.*

BELOW: *Based in Bridgwater, WebberBus was created in 1999 from an established family firm. A network of tendered and commercial services grew to cover much of Somerset, sparking fierce competition with First on some routes. In 2010 a seven-year contract was awarded to run the park-and-ride services in Taunton, but was terminated in 2014 due to poor performance. Heavy investment in new buses, many of them leased, resulted in a modern fleet of around 70 vehicles. Fourteen Optare Versas were operated, one of which was YJ62 FBL, pictured in June 2013 in the cathedral city of Wells working service 37 to Glastonbury and Street. WebberBus suddenly ceased trading in May 2016 after getting into financial difficulties.*

ABOVE: *The Silcox family of Pembroke Dock started running buses in the 1920s and became the dominant operator in the area, serving Pembroke, Tenby, Haverfordwest, and Milford Haven. A practice for many years was the re-bodying of second-hand double-deckers in its own workshops, but latterly the fleet was all single-deck, numbering around 70. Pictured in Carmarthen in August 2014 is UVG-bodied Dennis Javelin P780 WDE, having arrived on service 322 from Haverfordwest. Unsuccessful attempts to sell the business following financial problems led to its closure in June 2016.*

ABOVE: *Eastleigh-based Black Velvet Travel was formed in late 2007, commencing operations on local contract work and subsequently winning routes to Southampton, Winchester and Petersfield. Fleet strength peaked at around 20, evenly split between single- and double-deck. Trading simply as Velvet, one of the earliest acquisitions was 507 (V7 GMT), one of four ex-London Central DAF SB220s with East Lancs Myllennium bodywork, pictured in Eastleigh in October 2009 working service A to Boorley Green. At the start of 2014 cash flow problems began to manifest themselves and a proposed sale to Xelabus fell through. The company was sold to another buyer in July but operations ceased in January 2015.*

ABOVE: *Munro's of Jedburgh was founded in the mid 1960s but it wasn't until 2000 under new ownership that the business started to expand, building a network of services in the Scottish Borders stretching from Hawick to Berwick-upon-Tweed, and providing links north to Edinburgh and south to Newcastle upon Tyne. Fleet strength was around 30, and included the last pair of Optare Excels to enter service, as illustrated by 503 (YO53 OVA) in Melrose in June 2009 working service 68 from Galashiels to Jedburgh via Kelso. A cavalier approach to vehicle licensing brought the firm into conflict with the traffic commissioners and this, coupled with a major loss of contracts following re-tendering, prompted its sudden demise in July 2013.*

ABOVE: *John Fishwick & Sons of Leyland commenced bus operation in 1911 and for many years the services to Preston and Chorley were jointly worked with Ribble Motor Services. Leyland vehicles were the obvious choice in a mixed fleet of around 35 single and double-deckers. The last of the marque to be bought new was the Lynx, one of which, 4 (H64 CCK), is pictured sporting the traditional two-tone green livery as it leaves Preston bus station in September 2008 on the main 111 service to Leyland. Serious cash flow problems brought the business to a close in October 2015.*

BELOW: *Pennine Motor Services started in 1925 and for many years ran a lengthy joint service with Ribble from Skipton to Ingleton and Lancaster. Latterly the main services were to Settle and to Burnley, operated by around 15 single-deckers. The decision to close the business in May 2014 was partly due to competition from Transdev Burnley & Pendle and partly due to a reduction in the concessionary travel reimbursement provided by North Yorkshire County Council. Seen in Barnoldswick during the final week is ex-Bus Eireann Plaxton Pointer-bodied Dennis Dart D19 (W948 ETW), working service 215 from Skipton to Burnley.*

LEFT: *Western Greyhound commenced local services in 1998 and as First Western National retrenched in the 2000s the company grew to become the major provider in Cornwall, its network stretching from Land's End to Plymouth, with even one service to Exeter. At its peak awards were won for the quality of its operations, supported by a fleet of around 125, but in May 2013 an arson attack at the Summercourt depot proved to be a turning point, with increased insurance renewal costs severely draining finances. Seen in Newquay in July 2013 on service 586 from Truro is ex-Nottingham East Lancs-bodied Volvo Olympian 455 (S455 ATV). Routes were disposed of and the fleet downsized, but the sale to new owners in December 2014 failed to turn things around and services ceased abruptly in February 2015.*

ABOVE: *Formed in 1988, Bluebird of Middleton gradually built up a network of routes serving Manchester, Oldham, Bolton and Stockport with a fleet of around 45 single-deckers. Pictured in Oldham in March 2011 working town circular service 411 is Alexander Dennis Enviro200 EE56 BLU. The company was purchased by Stagecoach Manchester in March 2013.*

RIGHT: *In 1998 the Guildford-based Countryliner coaching unit inherited by Arriva from London & Country was sold off. Bus operation commenced in 2001 and services expanded beyond Surrey to reach places such as Hastings, Tunbridge Wells, Lewes, Brighton, Chichester and Petersfield, with the fleet size peaking at around 130, mainly single-deckers. Seen in Woking in May 2011 is MRM3 (AE56 MDF), an MCV Evolution-bodied MAN 12.220 on service 73 to Chobham. In 2009 skirmishes with HMRC were overcome but in 2011 financial concerns resurfaced and vehicle maintenance issues attracted sanctions from the traffic commissioner, forcing a contraction of the business. In October 2012 the Sussex arm of the company went into administration, with the Hampshire remnant following suit in January 2013.*

*The Barrow double-deck fleet in 1961 was made up entirely of Leyland Titan PD2s. 147 was new in 1950 and is seen with its original Park Royal body. Stuart Emmett collection*

# A SUMMER IN BARROW

**Stuart Emmett** recalls a holiday in Barrow-in-Furness in 1961.

As a young teenager in July 1961, I went from our home in Bradford to stay with my granddad in Barrow-in-Furness for three weeks. He lived on Beach Crescent at Biggar Bank on Walney Island. Walney is a small strip of land 11 miles long and mainly less than one mile across, and it shelters Barrow from the direct impacts of the westerly winds blowing off the Irish Sea. Barrow then had a population of around 70,000, with nearly 10,000 of them living on the largely residential Walney Island, especially in the part called Vickerstown, built to house workers at the local Vickers shipyard.

Barrow at the start of the 1960s was heavily industrialised, dominated by the large Vickers Armstrong Shipyard on Barrow Island.

The town is relatively flat, so many of the shipyard workers cycled to and from work, including going home for their lunch break. At the exit times from work, cyclists were commonly to be seen waiting and ready behind the shipyard gates. At the appointed time, the gates swung open and disgorged cyclists en masse in one whole block onto the roads. This immediately slowed down all other road traffic;

including the many workers' special buses.

Over 60 Barrow Corporation buses were required to run the regular services plus the workers' specials at peak times, when they carried around 5,000 people – and even more when it was wet and the bicycles were kept at home. Many of these workers' services turned short and did not cover the whole route. A maximum of just 34 buses were required for off-peak times, roughly from 8am to 5pm with a slight increase at lunch time.

BELOW: *The ten 1950 Titans were rebodied by Roe in 1959-60, apparently re-using the windows of the original bodies as can be seen on 149. Stuart Emmett collection*

ABOVE: *The last ten rear-entrance PD2s, delivered in 1958, had attractive four-bay Park Royal bodies. 162 is in Michelson Road bound for Tea House, with an appropriate advert on the side.* Stuart Emmett collection

As was noted in the Corporation bus timetable: "At the morning, lunchtime and evening peak periods, additional services will operate between the various termini and Vickers-Armstrong works." Ominously, the timetable also mentioned that "services operated especially for workpeople are liable to suspension if not needed".

Besides the main shipyard workers' specials for Vickers, there were also timetabled workers' services to the Lister's textile factory at Roose (a company with its main operation in Bradford), the ironworks, the hoopworks, the Cellophane factory and to the central railway station.

The main town terminus for all but one of Barrow Corporation's routes was around the Town Hall; the other terminus, for the joint Corporation/Ribble service to Ulverston via Dalton, was at Ramsden Square where, as we will see, other Ribble services terminated.

At peak periods, most of the mainland routes were extended back half a mile from the Town Hall area to serve the shipyard on Barrow Island. These were the services to Ormsgill, Cemetery, Hawcoat, Harrell Lane and Newbarns. The exception was the Ulverston via Coast Road route which, whilst it had timetabled workers' short running services to Roa Island and to Bardsea, none of these were shown in the 1961 timetable as being extended from the Town Hall to Vickers.

Meanwhile, the Tea House service to Roose already terminated near the shipyard on Barrow Island and the three routes out to Walney Island passed the shipyard in normal service. Finally, the Ulverston via Dalton route was extended from Ramsden Square to the Coffee House, this being near the Vickers yard.

## The routes

Barrow Corporation operated six town routes in the summer of 1961. There were no route numbers, but the final destination blinds were a different colour for each town route. The routes and colours were:

| | |
|---|---|
| Abbey to Biggar Bank | Green |
| Cemetery to North Scale | Black |
| Hawcoat to Newbarns | Red |
| Ormsgill to Harrel Lane | Yellow |
| Rainey Park to Harrel Lane | Yellow |
| Roose to Tea House | Blue |
| Barrow to Ulverston via Dalton | - |
| Barrow to Ulverston via Coast Road | - |

• The two Harrel Lane services operated as a circular route.
• The service to Ulverston via Dalton was operated jointly with Ribble.

## The fleet

In 1961 Barrow Corporation Transport had a relatively standardised fleet of Leylands in a livery

LEFT: *The fleet's three single-deckers were elusive. 52 was a Massey-bodied Leyland Royal Tiger.* Stuart Emmett collection

of navy blue and cream. There were 60 double-deck PD2 Titans which had entered service with Park Royal bodies, along with three single deckers, two Royal Tigers and a Tiger Cub. Between 26 and 34 buses were required for the normal timetabled services, the balance being used for workers' specials and maintenance cover.

The PD2s came in batches, by registration, of 12 and 18 in 1949; 10 in 1950, 10 in 1951 and 10 in 1958. The first 50, delivered between 1948 and 1951, were numbered from 111 to 160 and replaced 38 Leyland Titans which had been new between 1938 and 1942 along with 11 utility Daimlers and Guys from 1942-43. Titans 111 to 160 had identical bodies by Park Royal but with some small detail differences.

All of the PD2s were 8ft wide and gave Barrow one of the largest municipal fleets of 8ft-wide double-deckers at the start of the 1950s. The 1950 batch, 141 to 150, were re-bodied by Roe in 1959 whilst the final ten in 1958, numbered 161 to 170, had a totally different design of four-bay Park Royal body of a style introduced in 1954.

The three single-deckers were always elusive and were reportedly used as one-man-operated buses on the sparsely-populated Ulverston Coast Road service. I never saw them there when we regularly went to the Coast Road to visit relations in Rampside,

Goadsbarrow and Aldingham. The only place I ever saw them were at the 1936 depot in Hindpool Road.

## A ride to Biggar Bank

We always arrived at Barrow by British Railways from Carnforth; a most pleasant journey that went along the coast into Ulverston on what is now called The Lake District Peninsula. Just after Roose, close to Barrow, the town's industry came into view with sidings full of railway wagons and the shipyard cranes on the horizon. After alighting at the central railway station, a short walk took us into Abbey Road; this being the main A590 from Dalton and Ulverston.

We crossed Abbey Road to wait for the Biggar Bank bus to come down from the former tram terminus at Abbey, around 1½ miles away. The Biggar Bank bus – inevitably a PD2 in 1961 - then went down Abbey Road to Ramsden Square, from where Ribble's services operated to Ambleside (routes 517, 520), Ulverston (526/7) and Ulverston via Dalton (534, run jointly with Barrow Corporation). All of these were operated by single-deckers, apart from the 534 which was covered by Leyland Titan PD2s. Ribble's garage was at Ulverston, ten miles north-east of Barrow.

Continuing along Abbey Road for Biggar Bank, we turned left at Ramsden Square into Duke Street and were soon at the Town Hall. After a short wait, we then set off for the final two miles and turned right to go over the High Level Bridge. This had an 80ft opening section with docks on either side. On the left in Buccleuch Dock it was common to see grey Royal Navy frigates and destroyers being cannibalised or refurbished, while on the right in the Devonshire Dock there were often submarines.

After the bridge, we passed between many of the large engineering sheds owned by Vickers, which all

## Summer 1961 fleet summary

| 50 | EO 9765 | Leyland Royal Tiger PSU1/13 | Leyland B44F | 1952 |
|---|---|---|---|---|
| 52 | BEO 397 | Leyland Royal Tiger PSU1/13 | Massey B43F | 1955 |
| 53 | EEO 468 | Leyland Tiger Cub PSUC1/1 | Massey DP39F | 1959 |
| 111-122 | EO 8890-8901 | Leyland Titan PD2/3 | Park Royal H32/26R | 1949 |
| 123-140 | EO 9050-9067 | Leyland Titan PD2/3 | Park Royal H32/26R | 1949 |
| 141-150 | EO 9171-9180 | Leyland Titan PD2/3 | Roe H31/28R | 1950 |
| 151-160 | EO 9502-9511 | Leyland Titan PD2/3 | Park Royal H32/26R | 1951 |
| 161-170 | CEO 948-957 | Leyland Titan PD2/40 | Park Royal H33/28R | 1958 |

• 141-150 had been built with Park Royal bodies and were rebodied by Roe in the winter of 1959-60.
• 147/8 and 159/60 had platform doors for use on the service to Ulverston via Dalton

ABOVE: *Bicycles were popular with shipyard workers. Titan 132 threads its way through a throng of cyclists.* Stuart Emmett collection

ABOVE: *Shipyard workers heading towards the Town Hall on the High Level Bridge in 1957. The Vickers engineering sheds are in the background.* Stuart Emmett collection

seemed to be connected by the shipyard's own railway network. We then went on past the Coffee House and some Glasgow-style tenement homes. At the crossroads we turned right for Walney onto Bridge Road and just before the crossroads, Farm Street on the left took the route from Roose to Tea House, a further quarter of a mile away.

Bridge Road continued through the Vickers shipyard buildings and paralleled the internal Vickers railway. On the left was the slipway for the new ship builds; I saw *British Prestige* a tanker for BP, launched in July 1961, and had also seen the year before HMS *Dreadnought*, a Navy nuclear submarine, being launched into Walney Channel; quite a sight.

At the end of Bridge Road we turned left onto Jubilee Bridge with its 120ft opening over the Walney Channel, and ran onto Walney Island. Sometimes delays took place here when the bridge was opened to allow smaller ships, such as yachts with tall masts, to pass, as the channel to the north side was not very deep.

There were three roads at the end of Jubilee Bridge. Straight across, Central Drive ran up to the north side of Vickerstown and this road was used by the Rainey Park service from Harrel Lane. Along the road to the right, the Promenade, went the buses from Cemetery headed for North Scale. To reach our destination, now only about a mile away, the bus turned left on the Promenade, giving us a good view back across Walney Channel to the shipyard slipway.

We would soon climb up about 20 feet from the Promenade, and turn right onto the aptly named Ocean Road, which passed on the southern side of Vickerstown. Then it was back down to just above sea level to what was locally called the Gulley's (Tummer Hill Marsh being the official name). This area filled up with sea water from the twice daily tides, and with the high tides and a strong wind you could find a flooded road.

Biggar Bank terminus could be seen straight ahead

on the slightly uphill horizon some 40 feet above sea level at the top of Ocean Road (and at the end of the A590), but we soon swung left off Ocean Road, on the road to Biggar village on the Walney Channel side of the island. Then after about 50 yards, we turned right into Beach Crescent where we alighted at the bottom bus stop, and the bus continued to the top stop on Beach Crescent, before turning right at the T junction to reach the sea view terminus.

Biggar Bank was a quiet oasis most of the year, with only the Pavilion café, an open-air walled swimming pool, and some children's swings and paddling pools. That was it, except for the miles of unspoilt natural scenery and views out over the Irish Sea and north up to Black Combe mountain beyond Millom on the south western edge of the Lake District. On a clear day, the Isle of Man was visible, as was the black smoke trailed by the funnels from the distant ships and ferries. The beach was about 100 yards away down from the road over the grass, and at most times, the strong incoming prevailing westerly winds drove in the waves, leaving at low tides a good sandy beach with many rock pools. On sunny days, Biggar Bank was a common place to visit, especially at summer weekends when it could become very busy with day-trippers. ■

BELOW: *A mid 1950s view of Bridge Road with Barrow Corporation buses awaiting shipyard workers.* Stuart Emmett collection

MAIN IMAGE: *Close to Biggar Bank terminus, 149 drops off passengers in Beech Crescent. This is a 1950s view, before the bus was rebodied by Roe. Shipyard cranes are visible in the distance. Omnibus Society*

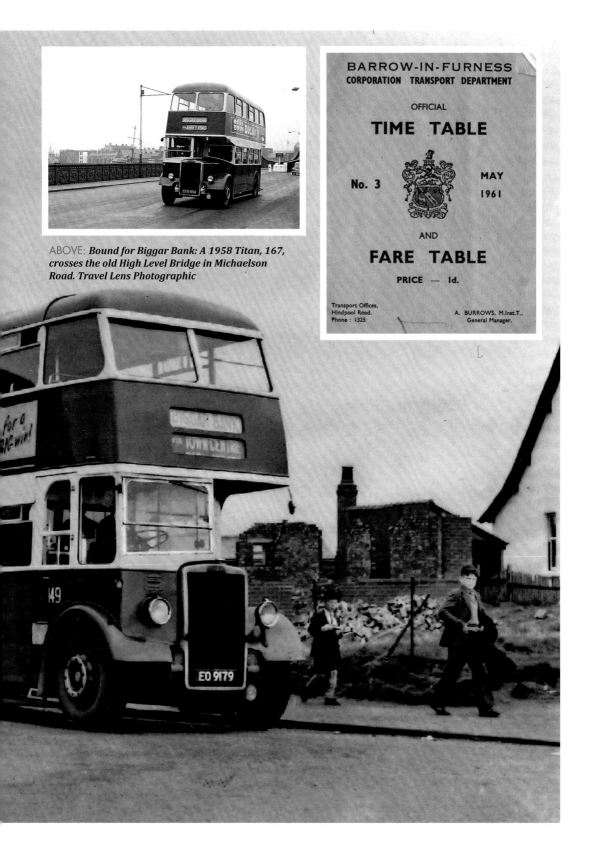

ABOVE: *Bound for Biggar Bank: A 1958 Titan, 167, crosses the old High Level Bridge in Michaelson Road. Travel Lens Photographic*

**BARROW-IN-FURNESS**
CORPORATION TRANSPORT DEPARTMENT

OFFICIAL

# TIME TABLE

No. 3                    MAY
                         1961

AND

# FARE TABLE

PRICE — Id.

Transport Offices,
Hindpool Road.                    A. BURROWS, M.Inst.T.,
Phone : 1325                      General Manager.

# A NORTH & MID WALES MISCELLANY

**John Young** looks at buses in Wales.

ABOVE: *Caelloi jointly operates service 3 (Porthmadog to Pwllheli via Criccieth) with Arriva Cymru. Its Optare Tempo is seen arriving in Pwllheli in July 2013.*

B us operations in Wales are having a torrid time. Reduced passenger numbers due to changing lifestyles, unabated growth in on-line retail, an elderly population that is more likely to be able to drive for longer and increasing traffic congestion are just some of the challenges.

Several operators have closed their doors for the last time, in some cases through retirement where no willing family successor or buyer has been found, but in others due to regulatory action or simply because of the harsh financial climate.

This collection of views over the last decade or so illustrates some of the many changes that have taken place. The tour starts at Pwllheli, working eastwards along the coast towards the English boundary then inland following the TrawsCymru T3 route to Dolgellau, before continuing south towards Ceredigion. ∎

ABOVE: *Nefyn Coaches operates a small number of services in the Llyn Peninsula. A Mercedes-Benz Vario with Plaxton Beaver body prepares to set out to Llithfaen in July 2013.*

ABOVE: *Groeslon is now a quiet backwater after trunk road improvements. One of a pair of rare Marcopolo-bodied MAN 18.220 saloons from the Express Motors fleet contributes to what was their main line service 1 (Bangor/ Caernarfon – Porthmadog – Blaenau Ffestiniog) in July 2014. Express Motors started out in a small way in the 1970s but expanded significantly much more recently, including taking on responsibility for former Silver Star routes in November 2010.*

ABOVE: *After a period of domination by Bristol LHs, Silver Star operated a mixed fleet of midis and minis. An ex-Stagecoach Alexander Dash-bodied Dennis Dart has just set out from Caernarfon for Talysarn in July 2010. Silver Star stopped running buses later that year.*

ABOVE: *Griffiths of Port Dinorwig closed down when the proprietor retired. Several Bristol VRs were operated on Gwynedd school contracts. This ex-Crosville example is seen at the operator's base and is now preserved in Crosville Cymru livery.*

ABOVE: *In North Wales' answer to colourful Tobermory and with mist evident at higher levels, Express Motors Optare Solo CX12 EMS passes along the main street in Llanberis bound for Bangor on 16 December 2017, just a fortnight before operations ceased. The operator's licence was revoked by the traffic commissioner.*

BELOW: *Padarn Bus was named after the lake in its home town of Llanberis. After some limited earlier forays in the tendered bus market, significant expansion came in April 2009 when it bought the parts of the KMP business that Arriva did not want. It closed down five years later in May 2014 amidst fraud allegations. An Optare Solo crosses Menai Bridge from Anglesey to Bangor on one of the supported services from the Beaumaris area.*

BELOW: *The Britannia Bridge provides the main link for Anglesey's bus services to reach the mainland. A lack of inter-timing can sometimes result in a procession of buses followed by a gap in service. Arriva Cymru received some cascaded early low floor Dennis Darts from the North East with traditional registration marks from the area. 2134 (S634 KHN) works in from Amlwch.*

ABOVE: *The coastal village of Dwygyfylchi is situated just off the main A55 between Penmaenmawr and Conwy. The modern day road layout is such that eastbound buses have to leave the village by initially heading back west to a roundabout to regain their natural course. An Arriva Cymru VDL SB120 with Wright bodywork disturbs the peace in January 2010.*

ABOVE: *Services from Chester to Rhyl benefited from investment by Arriva in a batch of ten Wrightbus Gemini 2 integrals. They reintroduced the Coastliner brand, originally synonymous with a fast hourly service along the coast, taking only three and a half hours to travel from Chester to Caernarfon. 4486 passes through Connah's Quay heading to Holywell (for Rhyl) in May 2012.*

BELOW: *GHA assumed responsibility for service X94 when Arriva Cymru withdrew the service and closed its Dolgellau depot. The route has its origins as Crosville's D94 which started out in 1965 as a rail replacement service. A Dennis Mini Pointer Dart passes through Corwen in July 2013.*

ABOVE: *Express Motors bought a new Optare Spectra in 2004. It served them well and was still in the fleet when the business closed at the end of December 2017 after investigation by the traffic commissioner. With Cader Idris looking down on Dolgellau's impressive architecture, the bus is about to depart Eldon Square on service 35 to Blaenau Ffestiniog, although displaying its ultimate linked destination of Llandudno, the entire journey passing through some magnificent scenery.*

BELOW: *In 2015 new investment came for the TrawsCymru service between Wrexham and Barmouth. Three Scania/ADL Enviro400s joined the GHA fleet and introduced regular double-deck operation to the route for the first time in its long history. The buses remain on the route today but are now operated by Lloyd's of Machynlleth.*

*The cottages, typical Welsh weather and chimney smoke create an atmospheric scene as a Dennis Dart SLF of the Lloyd's of Machynlleth fleet passes the cottages at Aberllefenni returning to Machynlleth, an attractive market town. Wyn Lloyd started his career at Mid Wales Motorways before moving to Crosville, eventually running Machynlleth depot which is the main base. In marked contrast to several other Welsh operators, Lloyd has gradually developed and expanded in a measured way and now covers a wide area, contributing significantly to the TrawsCymru network. Vehicles and staff are consistently well presented and punctuality is excellent.*

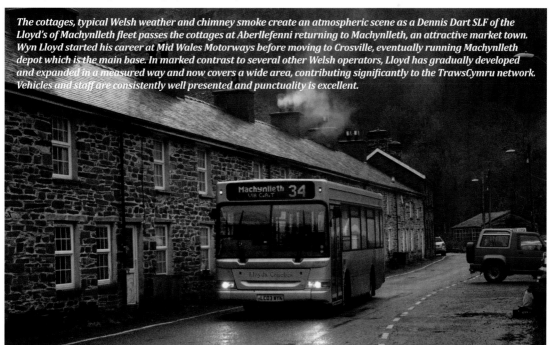

# COASTING ALONG

*Telscombe Cliffs form a dramatic backdrop to this view of a StreetDeck on its way to Brighton.*

All photographs by the author.

**Peter Rowlands** samples Brighton & Hove's high-frequency Coaster service.

magine a partially rural bus route that meanders along Britain's south coast for 22 miles – and is operated with high-capacity double-deckers at a frequency of every five to ten minutes. It's hard to believe – yet that's what you get with Brighton & Hove's route 12 group of services between Brighton and Eastbourne.

The service is not just intensive; it also has a very high profile, and covers some spectacular terrain. Not surprisingly, the operator, Go-Ahead subsidiary Brighton & Hove, has created unique branding for it (it's called the Coaster), along with a striking visual identity. Since 2015 it has been operated by long-wheelbase Wright StreetDeck integral double-deckers in a dramatic bright green and blue livery.

It's a far cry from the early 2000s, when there were complaints of late running and missed journeys, and it looked as though the service was in permanent decline.

A bit of context. Historically, the major country bus operator in the area was Southdown Motor Services, which dated back to 1915. Services between

Brighton and Eastbourne – two of the bigger resort towns in its area – were operated by the company from the early days, and by the postwar era route 12 had become firmly established.

However, in the mid-1980s, then state-owned Southdown was broken up and privatised, and for many years the route was shared by two successors to the divided company, Brighton & Hove and

BELOW: *A Coaster climbs out of Rottingdean towards Brighton.*

ABOVE: *Such is the frequency of buses on the 12 group of routes that they are often seen in pairs, though they usually diverge as those on the express version pass the stopping services. These two are seen arriving at Telscombe Cliffs.*

ABOVE: *Buses in overall advertising liveries sometimes appear on the 12. This five-year-old Volvo B9TL with Wright Eclipse Gemini body is seen crossing the Newhaven swing bridge in March 2018.*

Stagecoach. By then the service had gained an extra digit, becoming the 712.

Initially the standard buses on the route were Bristol VRs with Eastern Coachworks bodies inherited from Southdown, but Brighton & Hove soon began a long involvement with Scania, taking a batch of N113DRs with East Lancashire Coachbuilders' classic "droop-fronted" look.

Later Scanias included N113DRBs with East Lancs' much squarer Cityzen bodies. Then in 1999 came a batch of Dennis Tridents with East Lancs' similar-looking Lolyne bodies.

Stagecoach used more conventional buses such as Alexander-bodied Volvo Olympians, but in the 1990s it also introduced underfloor-engined Volvo Citybuses with Northern Counties bodies.

Then in 2005 Stagecoach closed down its operations in Eastbourne and the surrounding area, and Brighton & Hove gained full control of the route. Between 2004 and 2005 all versions of the service finally reverted to variants of the old number 12.

Ironically, Stagecoach re-established itself in Eastbourne four years later when it acquired the Eastbourne Borough Transport business; but it has not regained its share of route 12 to Brighton.

The revival of the route seems to date from the point when Brighton & Hove became the sole operator. The frequency was gradually increased, and more modern buses were acquired. Initially the company went back to Scania, and over the next few

BELOW: *A StreetDeck passes the level crossing in Newhaven on the Lewes to Seaford railway line.*

route is almost urban in character – especially the twelve-mile stretch between Brighton and Seaford. If you add up the populations of all the towns and villages along the entire route (but not those at either end), the total is probably not far short of 100,000 – the size of

years acquired several batches of N94 models with East Lancs' OmniDekka bodywork.

Then came the Wright StreetDecks. No fewer than 24 made their first appearance in 2015, and three more were added in 2017. These are seriously imposing vehicles, with a 10.5-metre wheelbase and a single-door configuration, providing space for 81 seats. The engines are Euro 6-compliant Mercedes-Benz OM934 5.1-litre units, which are coupled to Voith D854.6 four-speed automatic gearboxes. Passenger features include USB charging points on the upper deck, and on-board wi-fi by Icomera.

Like other buses in the fleet, those on the 12 carry names of well-known people who were connected with the area. Some of the latest names were chosen by public vote. Remarkably, around 500 people have been celebrated on Brighton & Hove buses since the scheme was launched in 1999.

How can the company justify such a strong commitment to this service? Basically, a lot of the

BELOW: *Seaford library is normally the turning point for the 12 from Brighton, but on this March morning in 2018, 929 was continuing through to Eastbourne.*

ABOVE: *A Scania OmniCity on the limited-stop X13 crosses the often congested mini-roundabout in the centre of Seaford in June 2017.*

a small city. No wonder the western part can seem almost continuously built-up, apart from a few short interruptions.

The route follows the A259 for almost its entire 22-mile journey, rising and falling with the contours of the coastline. Heading east out of Brighton, the first main settlement you encounter is the quaint, very upmarket (and very busy) village of Rottingdean, which feels like a tiny period town. Then there's an ascent and descent to the fringe of Saltdean, also upmarket, but inter-war suburban in character.

Another ascent and descent, then up to Telscombe Cliffs, which merges seamlessly into Peacehaven, a low-rise ribbon development that stretches for a couple of miles.

After a brief break, there's a descent into Victorian Newhaven, once a flourishing port, and still home to the Newhaven to Dieppe ferry service. Perhaps because of its past commercial and military significance, the town is much better known than

its neighbour, Seaford, even though these days it's barely half the size (maybe 13,000 residents compared with Seaford's 27,000).

There's a two-mile break between these two towns where the road runs between shallow cliffs on the north side and a narrow flood plain on the south. The river Ouse flowed along here until it was diverted in the sixteenth century to meet the sea at Newhaven.

Seaford, which once had pretensions of becoming a resort town, serves as a midway turning point for the 12. During the day, one in three of the journeys from Brighton (the 12 proper) terminates at Seaford Library in the centre of the town. However, two other variants of the service continue to Eastbourne, maintaining the promise of a ten-minute frequency over the whole route.

These are the 12A and the 12X, which offer two opposites in terms of service. The 12A meanders away from the A259 at several points – notably in Newhaven, where it visits the Paradise Park garden centre, and in Seaford, where it serves the Chyngton housing estate. By contrast the 12X, which was launched in 2008, operates on a limited-stop basis over the stretch between Brighton and Seaford, reducing the running time over the full route from

ABOVE: *A StreetDeck on the 12X waits at Eastbourne pier, ready for the return trip to Brighton.*

around 90 minutes to 75.

Beyond Seaford, the landscape changes dramatically, though the rise and fall of the terrain

*A far cry from today's high-quality vehicles, an ECW-bodied Bristol VR of Southdown with The Coastal Link branding stands at Eastbourne pier in April 1981. Behind it is a 1962 AEC Reliance of East Kent, originally carrying a Park Royal coach body, but rebodied by Plaxton in the early 1970s, and by this point converted for carrying disabled passengers.*

ABOVE: *Seen on Marine Parade, Brighton is a Scania N113DR with East Lancs bodywork. It was just two years old when photographed in May 1992.*

continues. There are sweeping vistas of rolling fields and clutches of woodland. Highlights include the meandering estuary of the Cuckmere river, and the open stretch just before Eastbourne, where the downland has an almost moorland-like quality.

Although you can't see them from the number 12 bus, the Seven Sisters white cliffs are just a short distance from this part of the route. Then just beyond them at the Eastbourne end is the area's most famous landmark, Beachy Head – the highest cliff of them all at 162 metres (531ft) above sea level.

On Sundays, and more regularly in the summer, an additional service, the 13X, shadows the 12X, but turns off the A259 towards Birling Gap and weaves its way over the downland to Beachy Head

before returning to the A259 route into Eastbourne. The 13X doesn't share the bounty of the Wright StreetDeck integrals; it uses buses in Brighton & Hove's standard cream and red livery – typically Scania OmniCity integrals.

At Eastbourne there's another route divergence. All versions of the service end up at or close to the sea front, but the 12X and 13X terminate at Eastbourne pier – as does the 12 proper, when it runs through to Eastbourne early on weekday mornings. The 12A, on the other hand, terminates half a mile to the west at the Winter Garden theatre.

Perhaps needless to say, over the years there have been many more variations to the 12 than there is space to cover here. At times single-deckers have appeared on the route, and there have been many tweaks to the route numbering. For instance, in 2003 some journeys were extended by three-quarters of a mile at the western end from central Brighton to Palmeira Square in the centre of Hove; but the change was short-lived, being dropped again in 2005.

The western terminus is now Churchill Square, Brighton, though up to 9am and after 7pm the route is diverted to and from Brighton station,

BELOW: *A Scania N113 with East Lancs Cityzen bodywork in Eastbourne in June 2002. One of the signs in the upper deck front windows offers a one-day saver ticket for £2.60. In 2018 the equivalent Network Saver is priced at £7 cash or £4.90 for an m-ticket.*

ABOVE: *This East Lancs Lolyne-bodied Dennis Trident carries the Metro branding used for some years by B&H. These were the first low-floor double-deckers used by B&H on the 712. It is seen in Seaford in June 2002.*

helping rail commuters.

Given that the 12 is such an intensive service, it has to contend with two conspicuous hold-up points along the way. One is in Newhaven, where the A259 encounters a pair of adjacent obstacles. It crosses the river Ouse on a swing bridge dating from 1974, which closes to traffic several times a month, causing significant delays.

Immediately next to this, the road crosses the Seaford to Lewes railway line via a level crossing, which closes frequently throughout the day. The rail crossing is bypassed by a flyover, which the limited-stop 12X magisterially uses, but the 12 and 12A have to take their chances at the level crossing down below.

The other hold-up point comes just east of Seaford, where the A259 crosses the Cuckmere river on a low-level single-lane bridge. Eastbound traffic has priority, but at busy times there

RIGHT: *A Stagecoach East Sussex Alexander-bodied Volvo Olympian seen on the last leg of its journey through Eastbourne in July 2002. It has coach seats.*

can be lengthy queues in both directions. It's a strange anomaly on a route that is so busy for much of the day.

Clearly the 12 group of routes has become a remarkable standard-bearer for the argument that high-intensity interurban bus routes can be operated successfully. But if you think this is long for a standard bus service, consider Stagecoach's related route 711, which was operated as recently as the 1990s. It ran from Brighton to Eastbourne, like the 712 and 12, then continued all the way through to Dover – a total distance of more than 90 miles. Journey time was more than five hours. You'd have to be pretty determined to sit that out very often. ∎

*This Volvo B10M with rare Van Hool service bus bodywork was acquired by Henderson in 1991 from Hutchison of Overtown and is seen in East Kilbride in 1993 on the service to Hamilton. It had been new in 1984.*

# THREE DECADES OF HENDERSON TRAVEL

Henderson Travel operated buses in west central Scotland from 1983 to 2014. **Billy Nicol** illustrates a selection.

*Two Willowbrook Warrior rebodied Leyland Leopards were purchased in 1991. The vehicle on the left had previously been with the Ministry of Defence; that on the right started life with Midland Red.*

ABOVE: *In the early days of Henderson's operations Mercedes-Benz minibuses dominated. This is an Alexander-bodied 709D which was bought new in 1996. It is in East Kilbride bus station.*

BELOW: *A bigger Mercedes purchased new was this O405 with Optare Prisma body, which joined the fleet in 1998. It was sold to Black Prince of Morley in 2001, and bought back in 2005. This photograph was taken when the bus was new.*

ABOVE: *This Leyland Leopard with Alexander T-type body carried dedicated school bus livery. It was new to Alexander Northern in 1980, but reached Henderson by way of Islwyn Borough Transport.*

ABOVE: *Henderson bought almost 50 new Optare Solos between 2000 and 2013. The first, a 33-seat M920 model bought new in 2000, is leaving Hamilton bus station for east Kilbride in 2002 in a livery commemorating the queen's golden jubilee.*

LEFT: *Prior to standardising on the Solo, Henderson bought a few Optare MetroRiders. This bus, new in 2000, is seen in Glasgow in 2003.*

BELOW: *A number of Leopards with Alexander Y-type bodies were operated. This bus was new to Alexander Fife in 1982 and is seen in Hamilton bus station in 2003, a testimony to the longevity of Leyland Leopards.*

ABOVE: *The first Optare Tempo for a Scottish operator was delivered to Henderson in 2006. It is seen when new leaving Glasgow's Buchanan Bus Station. The crisp carmine and cream livery was specified by SPT, the Strathclyde Partnership for Transport, for vehicles used on on SPT contracted services. It was also used on some suburban trains in the Glasgow area.*

BELOW: *In 2008 The Green Bus branding was adopted for buses which were deemed to be more environmentally-friendly, such as this Optare Solo M780SE, delivered in January 2008. It is leaving Glasgow for Torrance, a village eight miles to the north.*

ABOVE: *In later years Henderson adopted a silver-based livery, as illustrated by a 2010 ADL Enviro200 in Airdrie operating the long route 47A to Kirkintilloch and Milngavie.*

BELOW: *SPT later adopted an orange and grey livery for contracted services. This Fiat Ducato with Bluebird body is operating a MyBus demand-responsive service in Wishaw in 2012. It carries the Henderson Travel name on the bonnet and the first side window.*

ABOVE: *A larger bus in SPT colours was this ADL Enviro300, photographed leaving Hamilton for East Kilbride in 2013. It was new in 2008.*

BELOW: *One of the final deliveries to the company was this Optare Solo SR in December 2013. It was a 32-seat M900 model and was photographed at Monklands Hospital in April 2014. Henderson closed six months later, in October.*

# ATLANTEANS, ARTICS AND ARROWS...

All photographs by the author.

...and more besides as First tried to establish its corporate image in Southampton, observed by **David Jukes.**

ABOVE: *Four low-floor Plaxton Pointer-bodied Dennis Dart SLFs were purchased by Southampton Citybus in September 1996, all bearing this smart livery based upon that carried by an earlier demonstrator. 406 (P406 KOW) carried the FirstGroup logo on its nearside front window when photographed in Pound Tree Road in October 1997.*

Standardisation was effectively an unwritten requirement for Southampton's municipal bus operations after World War II. A large Guy Arab fleet, acquired between 1948 and 1954, was largely succeeded by the AEC Regent V.

The rear-engined Leyland Atlantean made its Southampton début in July 1968, with no fewer than 175 similar-looking East Lancs-bodied PDR1 and AN68 examples acquired new until 1982, with the type forming the entire Southampton City Transport fleet from 1981 for three years.

## Changing Times

But times were changing as four next-generation vehicles were delivered for trial purposes in 1984 as an Atlantean successor was sought. These appeared in the shape of one Dennis Dominator and three Leyland Olympians, all bodied by East Lancs. More of both types followed before and after deregulation in 1986, the latter to the council-owned arms-length company, Southampton Citybus Ltd.

The 1990s saw the company's sale to its management and employees on 21 December 1993, and most of the post-Atlantean double-deck

acquisitions were prematurely sold – just the original Dominator and two dual-purpose Olympians were retained. Replacements arrived in the shape of older Roe-bodied Atlanteans from Plymouth Citybus. Five indigenous Atlanteans were rebodied by East Lancs

BELOW: *The new order was evidenced by the painting of several vehicles in overall red with CityBus fleetnames and FirstGroup logos. 255 (YRV 255V), a 1980 East Lancs-bodied Leyland Atlantean, is seen in Shirley High Street in December 1997 alongside white-liveried 291 (P291 KPX), a 1996 Northern Counties-bodied Volvo Olympian purchased from dealer stock.*

with single-deck Sprint bodies in 1991. New Leyland Lynxes, Dennis Darts (diesel and gas-powered) and Volvo Olympian deliveries made further inroads into the Atlantean fleet.

## Into FirstBus

Southampton Citybus was sold to FirstBus on 28 July 1997. First CityBus, as the operation was named, inherited a mixed fleet of ten Leyland Lynxes, two Volvo B10Bs, five Roe-bodied Atlanteans, 76 East Lancs-bodied Atlanteans (including the five rebodied

ABOVE: *Southampton Citybus built up a sizeable school bus operation which was continued by FirstBus. Newly-repainted 271 (FTR 271X), a 1981 East Lancs-bodied Leyland Atlantean, carries the then-standard red livery with an added yellow band and SchoolBus fleetnames. Despite the SchoolBus branding it is operating on a regular service in Shirley Road in 1998.*

BELOW: *Four 9.8m Plaxton Pointer-bodied Dennis Darts were acquired in autumn 1995 – three new and one after a very short spell with Blue Triangle of Rainham. All operated in plain white for at least two years until being painted red. 402 (N466 ETR) is seen outside Southampton railway station in 1998 operating the Fastlink service to the Red Funnel ferry terminal.*

BELOW: *267 (FTR 267X), a 1981 East Lancs-bodied Atlantean, uniquely carried this bold First Southampton fleetname on the front. It is seen in Above Bar Street in the summer of 1998 soon after being repainted.*

LEFT: *305 (G305 XCR), a 1990 Duple Dartline-bodied Dennis Dart, was converted by Southampton Citybus to run on compressed natural gas – its roof-mounted tanks are hidden by the cowling. It was one of six Darts painted for operation on the Unilink services run in partnership with the University of Southampton as seen in Pound Tree Road in November 1998.*

The corporate willow-leaf livery (better known as Barbie by many enthusiasts) made its Southampton début in 1998 when the first of 20 group standard Plaxton Pointer 2-bodied Dennis Darts entered service. Other vehicles received a new fleetname layout to suit: CityBus in smaller text above front wheelarches with the First logo writ large on front, sides and rear – although with variations as old, not-so-old and new fleetnames were occasionally mixed.

## First Southampton to First Hampshire

The First CityBus identity proved short-lived as First Southampton took its place later in 1998. A seven-strong batch of group standard Wright Renown-bodied Volvo B10BLEs were among the first vehicles to carry the new name.

Another new livery appeared in the autumn of 1998 with the introduction of Unilink-branded services for the University of Southampton using the six earliest Darts. These gas-powered buses wore corporate coloured stripes on a light blue base.

First chose to adopt shared management for its Southampton and Provincial operations from 26

ABOVE: *Southampton Citybus had five of its Leyland Atlanteans rebodied with East Lancs 35-seat single-deck bodywork in 1991. 353 (OJI 1873) was originally 201 (HTR 571P), a 1975 AN68/1R with East Lancs double-deck bodywork. It is seen in Pound Tree Road in February 1999, not long after being repainted.*

single-deckers), one Dominator, two Leyland Olympians, six Volvo Olympians, 53 Darts (16 gas-powered) and four low-floor Dart SLFs.

Several Atlanteans and Olympians were dedicated Schoolbus vehicles with yellow bands and appropriate fleetnames. Liveries varied on red-based themes, although the six Volvo Olympians and four long-wheelbase step-entrance Darts wore dealer-stock white – a livery that took a little while to disappear.

## Initial Branding

FirstBus ownership was evident from day one as the corporate f logo and FirstBus lettering were applied to rear and nearside front windows. Corporate-style CityBus and SchoolBus fleetnames also appeared on several Atlanteans and Lynxes, either fully or partially repainted or with new fleetnames simply replacing old ones. It was not a swift programme, and the Southampton Citybus fleetname took its time to vanish.

BELOW: *The only Dennis Dart to receive the short-lived London-inspired red livery with grey and cream relief was Plaxton Pointer-bodied 310 (L310 RTP).*

March 1999; the latter served Gosport, Fareham and Portsmouth – and Southampton. The net result was First Hampshire (although Southampton and Provincial local identities remained) and the renumbering of the Southampton allocation to remove fleet number duplication with 1000 added to the fleet numbers of diesel-powered vehicles and 2000 to the gas-powered Darts. The fleet then consisted of ten Leyland Lynxes, two Volvo B10Bs, seven Volvo B10BLEs, 56 Atlanteans (five single-deck), one Dominator, two Leyland Olympians, six Volvo Olympians, 53 Darts (16 gas-powered) and 24 Dart SLFs.

## More colour and variety

Things became more interesting and colourful once again. Twenty mid-life MCW Metrobuses were dispatched from First Capital from late 1999; these had been new to Bristol Omnibus, South Yorkshire PTE and London Transport. Liveries were mixed: overall red, red with grey skirt and red with grey skirt and cream band – the last a short-lived attempt to introduce a new standard livery for Southampton's buses which was not to one of FirstGroup's standard specifications.

One of the former Bristol Metrobuses was allocated to driver training and carried another livery variation of red with white relief. A further six Metrobuses followed from CentreWest but not all 26 of the ex-London Metrobuses would be used – just 16 were in service during mid August 2000 with the others in reserve or having been found defective and sold on. The final example survived into 2005.

Other early First Hampshire disposals were the surviving Dominator and the five single-deck Atlanteans, while the diesel-powered step-entrance Darts began migrating to the former Provincial operating area.

ABOVE: *Application of the red, grey and cream livery was superseded by the introduction of a secondary corporate livery for vehicles that lacked group standard interior layout, trim and finishes. Former First Beeline Leyland Lynx 2 1099 (K802 CAN) displays the new livery – but without the magenta fade vinyls above the skirt – in Pound Tree Road in 2001.*

The new millennium heralded the arrival of 16 new Alexander ALX400-bodied Volvo B7TLs which increased the number of corporate-liveried buses on Southampton's roads. Smaller additions were three leased Optare Solos in a pale green livery for the sponsored City Link free service between the city's railway station and Town Quay via the West Quay shopping centre. A single Dart was painted orange for the similar City Loop which also served the coach station and various leisure attractions in and around the city centre.

The first of 18 articulated Wright-bodied Volvo B7LAs made its long-awaited début in July 2000. The type's stay would be short – two were loaned to First London in 2001 before passing to First Manchester the following year, while the remainder were being damaged through grounding on traffic calming measures and were dispatched to Glasgow in 2004. They had been joined by two earlier Wright-bodied

*Two 1999 Wright Fusion-bodied Volvo B10LAs were received from First Glasgow in 2000. 129 (V609 GGB) is advertising a competing form of transport, the Central Group's taxis.*

ABOVE: *Overground branding for route 17/17A is carried by 804 (W804 EOW), a 2000 Alexander ALX400-bodied Volvo B7TL, seen in Vincent's Walk in March 2003.*

ABOVE: *Two dual-purpose ECW-bodied Leyland Olympians were received from First Bristol. 1286 (A756 VAF) is in Vincent's Walk in the spring of 2003. It had been new to Western National in 1983.*

Volvo B10LAs – from First Glasgow – in 2000; these were also sent elsewhere – one to Bath in 2002 and the other to Manchester in 2003.

Remaining longer on the south coast would be five Leyland Lynxes transferred from First Beeline in September 2000, two of which introduced the Lynx 2 to Southampton.

## Metro and Overground

Metro route branding was introduced to the busiest and most frequent services in early 2001. Coloured vinyls were applied to corporate-liveried Volvos and low-floor Darts plus red-liveried Lynxes and Atlanteans – the last complete with the yellow band applied for school duties. To balance this, the Southampton local identity fleetname began to disappear from vehicles as instruction was issued for the First logo to be the sole identifier.

Atlantean disposals continued with several surprisingly transferred within First for further service; five to Huddersfield in 2000 and three to Leicester in 2001. Dispatched for scrap were the six

earliest Darts (five of which had the second to sixth-built Duple Dartline bodies), converted from diesel to gas power between July 1995 and July 1996.

It was an Atlantean which caused further surprise in February 2002 when number 1264 – then 21 years old – was repainted in First's secondary vehicle corporate livery (the so-called Barbie 2), the sole example to be so adorned. Other types also received these colours – the original low-floor Darts, four Volvo Olympians (the other pair received overall advertisements), a few Lynxes and both Volvo B10Bs. The last were also treated to X27 route branding; the express service to Portsmouth was their usual haunt.

More colour was added in late 2002 and early 2003 with the arrival of 19 East Lancs-bodied Dennis Arrows from First London. Most were received in Capital Citybus yellow livery, although some were converted to single-door layout at Hants & Dorset Trim and painted in Barbie 2 colours. Some subsequent arrivals were in the later Capital Citybus livery which was predominantly red with yellow relief – some carrying both London and Hampshire fleet numbers in service.

Accompanying these were six second-hand Leyland Olympians in Barbie 2 livery: three full-height Roe-bodied buses and two low-height ECW-bodied dual-purpose machines from First Bristol and a single full-height Roe-bodied bus – complete with cherished registration – from First South Yorkshire that had originated with West Yorkshire PTE.

Metro was replaced by Overground in February 2003, although the new brand was only applied to vehicles in First's corporate liveries. The X27 service to Portsmouth was also upgraded with the arrival of two Plaxton Expressliner-bodied Volvo B10Ms in corporate Excel livery to replace the Volvo B10Bs, both of which were transferred to First Manchester.

## Into First Hampshire & Dorset

First merged its Hampshire and Dorset operations in 2003; the latter was essentially the deregulation-era Southern National acquired with Cawlett Holdings in 1999.

Five of the former Southampton Citybus Volvo Olympians were transferred to First Devon and Cornwall in 2003; the sixth moved to Manchester in 2004. First introduced its national fleet numbers to the south coast in early 2004. In January 2004 Tellings-Golden Miller took over operation of the X27 with its own vehicles.

The articulated Volvos were replaced by 19 ex-Stagecoach Group long-wheelbase Volvo

Olympians acquired after lease expiry – more standard-length examples followed as the Arrows took flight to Manchester in 2005, the same year the Atlantean, Lynx and Metrobus took their final bows – as did the ex-Southampton Citybus red livery.

The remaining gas-powered Darts, despite their relative youth, were out of use by the end of 2006 and dispatched for scrap the following year. Other remaining ex-Southampton Citybus stock would last longer – the two dual-purpose Leyland Olympians until 2009 and the four low-floor Darts until 2015.

The final example of the six ex-dealer stock Volvo Olympians purchased in 1996 was also withdrawn from Hoeford during 2015 – it returned south for a spell on First Hampshire & Dorset school duties after a decade in the West Country and Manchester. The final pair of step-entrance Darts, new in 1995, were both sold for preservation in February 2018 after use by First Hampshire & Dorset on an Eastleigh-based private contract, while the two Volvo B10Bs remain part of First West Yorkshire's driver training fleet at

the time of writing.

And that is probably a good place to stop. The accompanying pictures show several of the livery and fleetname combinations evident in Southampton between July 1997 and the introduction of national fleet numbers in early 2004. These kept my camera busy while resident in Shirley until late summer 2001, and thereafter when seconded back to the city for a three-year period just six months after moving away. ∎

BELOW: *301 (M41 FTC), a 1995 Plaxton Expressliner-bodied Volvo B10M, was one of two identical coaches transferred to First Hampshire in corporate Excel livery for route X27 linking Southampton and Portsmouth. It is awaiting departure from Pound Tree Road in September 2003.*

# THE CHANGING FACE OF NOTTINGHAM'S BUSES

Nottingham City Transport is widely acknowledged to be among Britain's best bus operators. **John Robinson** illustrates the changing fleet.

Nottingham City Transport is one of just nine remaining municipal operators and the second largest - after Lothian Buses - operating around 67 routes and 330 vehicles. Always an innovative operator in terms of vehicle design and models operated, this trend has continued with the phased introduction of 53 gas buses in 2017-18. Its traditional green and cream livery was superseded from September 2001 by colour-coded route-branding, whereby every bus route was assigned a colour, with all services leaving the city centre via the same route (or in the same general direction) having the same colour. Nottingham's other main operator, Trent Barton, is also a long-time user of route-branding meaning the city is a sea of colourful liveries, a far cry from how it looked prior to local bus deregulation over 30 years ago. ∎

LEFT: *Nottingham's first rear-engined double-deckers were Daimler Fleetlines which arrived in 1962, carrying Park Royal bodywork to the builder's standard design. The undertaking subsequently developed its own distinctive style of body for rear-engined double-deckers under the guidance of its chief engineer, John Lowrie, and this first appeared on a batch of Northern Counties-bodied Leyland Atlanteans in 1964. By 1966 the design had changed significantly and continued to be supplied, with various modifications, until 1982 on Leyland Atlanteans and 1988 on subsequent second-generation chassis. This view in Lower Parliament Street in April 1991 affords a comparison between the East Lancs bodies on 328 (E328 BVO), one of 15 Volvo Citybuses new in 1988 and 640 (ARC 640T), a Leyland Atlantean new in 1978.*

RIGHT: *The last Leyland Atlanteans were delivered in 1981-82 with batches bodied by both East Lancs and Northern Counties, and represented the final evolution of Nottingham-style bodywork on first-generation rear-engined double-deckers. 447 (ORA 447W) was one of ten with East Lancs bodies new in July 1981 and shows the bonded glazing fitted to these vehicles. It is in Long Row (now pedestrianised) in April 1991 operating service 58 to Killisick, a service which still operates under the same number as part of the Lime Line.*

ABOVE: *Nottingham set up a small coaching unit in 1980 when two Duple Dominant-bodied Leyland Leopards entered service, introducing a cream and brown livery to differentiate them from the buses. Later additions were two Duple-bodied Leyland Tigers, delivered in February 1985, numbered 784 and 794 which had Caribbean II and Laser 2 bodies respectively. 794 (B794 JAU) is seen leaving Blackpool's Coliseum Coach Station in June that year operating National Express service 952 back to its home city, a route the pair often saw service on.*

BELOW: *Nottingham first showed an interest in Scania products in 1981 when it purchased a double-deck demonstrator from the manufacturer; it is now by far the predominant make in the fleet and Scanias continue to be purchased in quantity. Two Alexander-bodied N113DRBs are seen in Angel Row in 1991. 370 (G370 RTO) is one of 18 new in 1989-90 whilst behind is 380 (F380 JTV), an additional vehicle acquired from Scania in 1989.*

ABOVE: *NCT purchased the Ilkeston depot of Stevensons of Uttoxeter in 1988 and set up a low-cost subsidiary trading as Erewash Valley. A number of buses were transferred to the new operation including 1974 East Lancs-bodied Leyland Atlantean E81 (OTO 581M), formerly fleet number 581, seen at the depot entrance in Hallam Fields Road, Ilkeston, in 1991. The 'Save our Shipstones' advert refers to the Shipstones Brewery in Nottingham which, despite the plea, closed early in 1991 after 139 years. This was one of seven Nottingham Atlanteans acquired by Strathclyde Buses the following year to replace some of the 60 buses destroyed in a fire at its Larkfield garage.*

ABOVE: *A total of 23 Optare Excels entered the fleet between 1996 and 2002. 556 (FD51 EYY) was one of eight new in December 2001 and January 2002 and is seen in Angel Row operating an evening 35 service to Bulwell via Wollaton Vale.*

RIGHT: *In 1997 NCT acquired Pathfinder of Newark, and retains the fleet name for its 100 service from Nottingham to Southwell. Scania N270UD/East Lancs OmniDekka 945 (YN08 MSO), one of four similar vehicles carrying Pathfinder branding, pulls out of the turning circle at the terminus in Norwood Gardens, Southwell, heading back to Nottingham in April 2018.*

*NCT took the UK's first proper batch of Scania OmniTowns in 2004 when seven entered service for use on tram feeder services. Remaining the only vehicles of this type in the fleet, the model comprised Scania's N94UB chassis with East Lancs Myllennium bodywork but the Nottingham ones were the first to incorporate Scania's distinctive front and rear ends on the Myllennium bodies. Later moving on to other duties, all are now in green spare livery, where they can be used across the network as required. Loading in Angel Row, 205 (YN04 ANP) works an evening Green Line service 11 to Lady Bay in February 2017.*

The only Optares in the current fleet are nine Solos and 34 Solo SRs. Eight SRs carry Bridgford Bus branding for Green Line services, seen in this view of 358 (YJ12 GYS) in April 2018 operating service 5 to Gamston heading out of the city along Arkwright Street.

ABOVE: *In 2013 NCT took delivery of 33 ADL Enviro200s, a new type for the fleet. Two are seen in this busy morning view in Lower Parliament Street in July 2017. 367 (YX13 AEJ) heads to Arnold on Purple Line service 87 via Sherwood, closely followed by 378 (YX13 BNV) on Brown Line service 16 to Rise Park.*

LEFT: *Two Enviro200s are allocated to Skyblue Line services 46/47 which go from the city via Mapperley Plains to Woodborough and Lambley, villages outside the city boundary, and passing through some of the most rural scenery served by NCT. 386 (YX63 LJC), illustrates this as it approaches Woodborough in April 2018 on the 47 which operates in an anti-clockwise loop through the villages; the 46 runs in the opposite direction. Services 46/47 originate from routes taken over by NCT following the collapse of Premiere Travel in January 2013.*

ABOVE: *A total of 62 Scania N230UD/ADL Enviro400s entered the fleet between 2013 and 2015. 629 (YN14 MUY) operating Orange Line service 36 to Chilwell via Queen's Medical Centre (the QMC in the destination display) and Beeston, waits in Angel Row on the evening of 16 February 2017 with the Wheel of Nottingham, a 60-metre high observation wheel located in Old Market Square, dominating the skyline. From April 2018 this route was converted to gas buses and its dedicated Enviro400s had the 36 branding removed and began operating on Orange Line service 35 to Bulwell.*

LEFT: *Seven of the Enviro400s carry South Notts branding. This well-known independent, based in Gotham, was taken over by NCT in March 1991. Its main route from Nottingham to Loughborough via Gotham and East Leake is now Navy Line service 1, this colour perpetuating the blue from South Notts' former blue, maroon and cream livery. 642 (YN15 EJC) heads along Carrington Street past the station in April 2018 on its way to Loughborough with two Trent Barton single-deckers in the background.*

The first of 53 bio-gas-powered Scania N280UDs with Alexander Dennis Enviro400 CBG City bodywork entered service in July 2017 on Green Line routes 6 to Edwalton and 10 to Ruddington. Further conversions followed that month on the Red Line (44 Gedling) and in August on Lilac Line (24 Westdale Lane and 25 Arnold). March 2018 saw Skyblue Line (45 Gedling) converted with the last 12 buses being allocated to Orange Line 36 to Chilwell in April. A bio-gas refuelling station was built at Lower Parliament Street depot where gas drawn from the national grid is compressed and stored until the buses are filled up each night.

ABOVE: *In April 2018 Green Line 405 (YP17 UFE) heads out to Ruddington past Nottingham's magnificent Edwardian Baroque Revival station frontage. The station was opened by the Midland Railway in 1904 to replace earlier buildings.*

*In Wollaton Avenue, Gedling, Red Line 417 (YP17 UGJ) approaches its terminus (just to the right out of frame) having arrived from the city via Colwick and Netherfield. Skyblue Line 440 (YN18 SVY) stands in the turning circle of the 45 service ready for departure to the city by the shorter route via Mapperley.*

*Orange Line service 36 was converted to gas buses on 16 April 2018. Two days later 444 (YN18 SXC) waits at the traffic lights under the tram wires in Market Street operating a late evening journey to Chilwell.*

ABOVE: *Whilst NCT embraces the newest technology it is also proud to celebrate its past. In June 2016 Scania N94UD/East Lancs OmniDekka 676 (YN05 WFE) was repainted into trolleybus livery to mark 50 years since the system closed on 30 June 1966. When photographed leaving Bulwell Bus Station on 18 April 2018 the lettering had been changed to 'Celebrating 140 years serving Nottingham 1878-2018'. It is operating the circuitous Turquoise Line service 79, from Victoria Centre to Arnold, which has a scheduled journey time of around 70 minutes, the longest route operated by NCT.*

BELOW: *Eight of the gas buses are painted in a generic silver spare livery so they can be switched between different lines as required. Typifying these is 426 (YP17 UFJ) picking up outside the station in Carrington Street operating Green Line service 6 to Edwalton (at that time the only gas bus service) during a downpour in July 2017. The low viewpoint to capture this reflection was achieved by holding the camera just above pavement level and composing the picture using the camera's live view function.*

# QUIET MOMENTS

Buses are not always hard at work. **Chris Drew** illustrates vehicles, and their drivers, at rest.

## Hushed Tones

ABOVE: *There is scarcely a town or village in the UK where a memorial cannot be found to the fallen from the wars of the 20th century, their names set in steel or stone for the generations to come to identify with. The scene here was in Norfolk Square, Glossop and bore all the hallmarks of a typical monument, with even the pigeons adding to the solemnity of the picture. Parked up on one side of the square in Henry Street was Greater Manchester 4001, one of the few new Leyland Titan TN15s to be found operating outside London. Not visible in the photograph because it was on the wall behind the Titan was a sign which requested that, 'No GMT buses to be parked below this sign' meaning the bus should have been parked at the stop provided. I think this driver must have been very eager to park up because he's ignored the request. Possibly it was an urgent call of nature. If 4001 had parked in the correct place, I would have found it impossible to frame it in this photograph. Despite all the scientific work put into this design the Titan wasn't well received. It was considered to be a 'one size fits all' type of bus which clearly was not going to work for everyone. Sales outside London were measured in penny numbers. Greater Manchester went on taking the trusty AN68 Atlantean until legislation killed it off and the Olympian replaced it. It turned out that to some operators, the Olympian was the bus that the Titan should have been in the first place.*

## Leafy

RIGHT: *Fairlight Glen is not as one might expect a meeting place for Highland clans, but a secluded terminus two miles east of Hastings at which is seen Maidstone & District's 3692, delivered as S192 in 1963. It was a Harrington-bodied AEC Reliance, unusual in being only 7ft. 6in wide. The driver takes a few of his precious minutes of peace and quiet to check and reset his ticket machine. As I had been the only the only passenger on the trip up, and a half fare at that, I think route 134 might have made a slight loss on that journey. Nearby is the beach at Covehurst Bay from which it's possible to walk back to Hastings: but beware, the shingle beach makes it an arduous trip plus high tides can cut off your retreat. For enthusiasts of a certain age (and I'm one) Maidstone & District's dark green livery was one that would be greatly missed when the National Bus Company took over.*

## Windless

BELOW: *The night was warm and still, perfect for riding a motorbike. I had been coming home from seeing a friend in Forest Row and my journey took me through East Grinstead heading for Godstone. I got as far as Felbridge and just happened to glance up a side road where I saw a London Country XF waiting for what was probably its last journey of the day. I turned around and went back and then realised that although I always carry a camera with me, I didn't have a tripod. I turned my engine off, undid my helmet and silence came flooding in. I saw the explosion of light from the cab as the driver went to strike a Swan Vesta against a box and lit up a cigarette. The blind was set for a return to East Grinstead only a few miles away, making this a very short run. With no tripod I rustled through the undergrowth to find a tree with a decent fork in it and clear line of sight for the shot. A car went past travelling north and then silence again. Camera set, just the sound of my breathing. Click...2....3....4....5....6...click. It's always fun doing a time exposure. Wind on, take another, went to wind on again, no give, out of film, no more in the bag. The object of my picture, XF1, sat waiting while its driver pulled a final drag on his Wills Woodbine and left. Replaced my camera in its safe place, turned on the ignition, pushed the starter and drove away in a crescendo of four-stroke noise. That group of eight Fleetlines had always been a favourite of mine and this, as it turned out, was to be the last time I saw one in the wild but my thoughts went back to a Green Rover ticket I bought in the 1960s which allowed me to travel on the 424 from East Grinstead to Reigate, their spiritual home when they were new.*

## Delicate pearl like stone

RIGHT: *I'm lucky that I grew up in a family which loved travelling. When I got married, I was lucky to find someone who not only liked roaming the country but positively adored being a passenger on as many different forms of transport as she could. When a chance came up to travel the Settle to Carlisle line behind a Gresley A4 steam engine we jumped at it. At the northern end Carlisle station struck me as a most imposing structure. It was built in 1847 in a Neo-Tudor style to an original design by William Tite. Waiting in front of the station to return on its Scottish Borders Rail Link service was Lowland's Leyland Tiger 323. This bus was ordered by Scottish Omnibuses and delivered to them in December 1983 as ZL323. It carries Alexander's TE-style 49-seat bodywork, a good looking, balanced design, far better than the original T with its stepped roof line. The driver sits on the entrance step, catching up with the news in the break between his journeys.*

## Catch up with friends

LEFT: *A quiet moment just to reacquaint oneself with a friend or pass the gossip on to a neighbour or just give a family member the bottle of milk bought earlier. I'm not sure which this lady talking to the driver was, but she was there before Cornish Busways Mercedes minibus 65 arrived at Truro garage and she was still there after it had left on its way to Three Mile Stone, presumably via One Mile Stone and Two.......oh never mind!*

## The quiet before the storm

RIGHT: *The scene, Snape Maltings, Suffolk, one of the UK's leading centres of musical excellence, founded by Benjamin Britten, the Suffolk-born composer. It's not only used as one of the venues for the Aldeburgh Festival but also has its own array of independent shops, cafes and art galleries. This is all set in redeveloped Victorian industrial buildings nestling where the B1069 crosses the River Alde. That's the advert over and done with, but it's why these two Sullivan buses are there. The Dennis Trident on the left and the Volvo B7TL on the right, both bodied by East Lancs, have each brought a full manifest of passengers from different areas to the north of London. Having completed the initial part of their job, they wait quietly against the background of an industrial facade for the mass of well fed, well shopped and well tired visitors to return.*

**Boredom**

*The sound of breath being expelled through teeth. Just enough time to do the crossword. The location was the coach pick-up point located under the then new office and shopping complex built over the throat of London's Victoria Station. Towards the late afternoon, commuter coaches would gather there ready to make their dash for destinations in Surrey, Kent or Essex. It had an air of the mass departures from Cheltenham's coach station, except slower. On the day this photograph was taken I arrived early and apart from the driver and myself, there was nobody to be seen. This and the cool temperature in the tunnel lead to a Third Man-style very uneasy feeling. Other coaches began to arrive and find a space to pick up, then ... as if a school bell rang, people were rushing about in all directions like uncoordinated ants. The driver of this DAF MB230 with Van Hool bodywork whipped open the door and within what seemed minutes the coach was nearly full and leaving for Kent.*

## Unhurried

LEFT: *I watched this scene unfold as I waited for my bus. The young lady was waiting for a friend who was late. She explained to the driver about her friend but the driver seemed anxious to be on his way. His Kent Karrier Omni was prepped and ready to leave Tonbridge for pastures new and leave pretty soon as well. The driver had opened the doors a minute before in the hope of encouraging her on board. She was having nothing of it and it soon became a round of call my bluff. When the friend arrived seconds later the girl roundly chastised her for embarrassing her with the driver. The doors clattered shut and the happy crew steamed off down towards the station. I never really could work out who actually won the game.*

## Relief

BELOW: *Touring all day with a nice bunch of people is all right, but they can still be hard work. The driver of Elcock Reisen, (why the German I wonder?) chats to the last few of his charges from the day, before he reboards his Plaxton-bodied Volvo B10M, wanders back to the depot there to clean and check it for the next day. Elcock is Ironbridge's home company. It's interesting to compare the logo with the real thing in the background. They were founded in 1928 and have grown along with Coalbrookdale, recognised as the cradle of the industrial revolution, which has become a heritage site and tourist centre. The Volvo shows the high standards to which the fleet is kept.*

## Time to catch up

RIGHT: *Passengers also have quiet moments whilst waiting for their transport to arrive. This young man is topping up his knowledge while a Limebourne Dennis Dart gently ticks quietly to itself. When the driver reappears, it will relocate the waiting youth from Wimbledon to somewhere else down route 156. Once upon a time a well respected coach firm in the city, Limebourne was one of an adventurous group of coach operators who tried running contracts for London Regional Transport. Limebourne's fleet was made up of brand spanking new Dennis Darts with either Plaxton or Caetano/UVG bodywork in a red livery with a grey skirt and green square emblem with the name across it. By autumn of 1998, Limebourne was in trouble. The company that owned it, Q-Drive, went into receivership in the October. By November the Limebourne management had bought the company out but this all took too long for the leasing companies who quickly repossessed their vehicles leaving the new company, Limebourne (Independent Way) without a bus. To their credit, they did manage to pick up some second-hand Dennis Darts quickly but the writing was well and truly on the wall, possibly the same wall that Limebourne's managers had their backs to.*

## Ultimate peace

BELOW: *Such is life; death comes to all. Although I didn't realise it when I took the photograph, this bus was quite a star. It was delivered to Eastern Counties in February 1949 and instantly along with another 189 Bristol Ks from other Tilling Companies was hired to London Transport to cover a gap in the fleet. It spent an uneventful time at Clay Hall garage in Bow until March 1950 when it was time to come home to East Anglia. It was however, unusual in being a highbridge version which was in the minority of buses loaned to London. It was numbered LKH121 in the Eastern Counties fleet and spent the next the next 18 years earning revenue for the company until one day in 1968 it was sold via dealer Ben Jordon to Anglian Canners of Kings Lynn whose name was still visible in the blind box. It had already begun to be stripped of bits and pieces when I found it at a scrapyard at Thorney between Peterborough and Wisbech in Cambridgeshire.*

# SHADES OF SIX DECADES

**Robert E Jowitt** reflects on photography with, in his usual style, deviations from the main subject.

ABOVE: *Parisian Paradise. Barring a few details of bodywork the silhouettes of the buses in this 1970 scene could have been seen at any time in the preceding half-century, but actually here in the final fling of the existence of the faithful 1935 Renault TN4F. with only weeks to live. Paris could never be the same thereafter.*

Recently, in writing a mildly commemorative little article for the Friends of King Alfred Running Day programme regarding the passage of time and how little we can actually save from such onslaught, I fell to meditating on the fact that in the summer of 2018 it was 60 years since I took my first PSV photograph and how since the world has changed again and again.

Aged 16, I was staying with a Westphalian pen-friend, and was conveyed perilously and helmet-less by her father on an inefficient scooter to Paderborn, presumably to sample the annual festival including fairground ghost trains with decorations of such Hieronymus Bosch horror that I could hardly look at them. I expect we inspected the bubbling springs of the River Pader and the window at the cathedral depicting the three rabbits or hares with only three ears between them. What I had not known before, I think, was that Paderborn boasted trams

of considerable antiquity. Unable to find any picture postcards displaying their likeness I photographed them instead. I wonder whether had I found a postcard I might not have bothered and therefore where might I be now!

These Paderborn photos were almost what would now be deemed record shots but the seed had been sown. Over the following year, 1959, I was already – by instinct I must suppose – starting to add architecture, crowds of humans, artistic curlicues of track, and huddles of trams and buses the more together the better. Frankfurt am Main in heavy rain proved a particular inspiration; Sheffield remarkably without rain likewise, though in both cases I was admittedly trying to capture as many different types of tram as possible. Belgium and the Netherlands proved classic tramway paradise, plus Germany with repeat visits to Paderborn and the equally archaic Koblenz.

Then in 1960 came greater enlightenment and

On the banks of the Saone, with fang-like post-war blocks crowning the cliffs on the opposite shore, Lyon ran nearly 150 Berliet VA3B2, of 1954-60, heftiest of all French trolleybuses, carrying 111 passengers (with only 23 seated). The 1969 photo shows the French system (not universally employed) of fleet number in place of registration number, presumably on the happy assumption that the trolleybus was captive under its own city's wires.

inspiration, the tenements of Glasgow, four or more floors of bleak housing hemming tramlines with splendidly archaic trams and trolleybus besides, and then atmospheric housing not dissimilar plus a very impressive trolleybus presence in St Etienne and Lyon, France. To which I have to add the truly heroic antique buses of Paris. A year or so later I found Vienna near as good as Glasgow and Innsbruck near as good as what I care to guess heaven might be. Meanwhile, as a student at Bournemouth College of Art, there came an intensive study of every part of the Bournemouth Corporation Transport trolleybus system, surely an art form itself.

The so-called Swinging Sixties – in which in the early years we young people thought we were likely to be nuked out of existence at any moment, so grabbed every moment in diverse desperate pursuits – were marked by major removal out of existence of the

greater part of British trolleybus systems and a quantity on the continent too. As many of all these as possible did I chase, and the more I did so the more I developed the theme that it was not just a boring bus that was required; it was the boring bus being an enlightener and serious partaker in its own home scene.

What occupied me most in the late 1960s was the approaching final demise of those Paris Renaults, including my efforts to buy one and then another for preservation ... but most of you know all that oft-related tale. Nevertheless I was busy whenever

RIGHT: *Glasgow tenements form a backdrop to a Corporation BUT trolleybus with London-style Metro-Cammell body.*

LEFT: *In my youth I somewhat deplored the RM as usurper of RTs and trolleybus from the streets of London, but learned to love it is an 'icon of the capital', still thriving decades after introduction, as depicted on Oxford Street in the 1990s.*

opportunity offered in pursuit of trams and trolleybuses in Switzerland, Northern Italy, Spain and Portugal. Iberian hunting – including London trolleybuses in Spain and AECs in Portugal continued now and then until 1984 (was Big Brother watching me?), but I sometimes feel my most creative decade was 1966-76. This of course was partly because the available material was, bar waning Paris, still plentifully laden with the charm of years… though like Paris waning too!

This is not to say, of course, that my powers diminished later with less receptive subjects. Well, it is my ardent hope and belief that they didn't! Through the 1970s and 1980s I was in Winchester witnessing the bizarre patchings-up which followed the death of King Alfred, notable here a brief attack by two ex-Sheffield Leyland articulateds, soon at death's door. About now I began to be encumbered by divine offspring, (my daughter's earliest memories include riding on one of these articulateds, rather more clearly than memories of her granny) such as are less easy to abandon than dogs or Paris buses, so thenceforth, barring a last hunt for the once-reviled but now adorable French Saviem standards, and abandoning Hampshire for Herefordshire, I found myself restricted to more immediate gems such as Bristol, Birmingham, Manchester and, once, for a few glorious days, Edinburgh. Anyway for shortness of the needful I was earning a living driving buses in the Welsh Marches, glorious country, sometimes utterly horrible school brats. I have often noticed on widespread travel that 'kidz' let out from education onto public transport lose any sort of notion of decent behaviour. If they ever had any.

The house in the Borderlands was too big to heat, and in the winter-icy bed of what had in prehistoric

times been a lake, and too isolated; with extreme reluctance (on my part) we fled to the warmer and more child-friendly Isle of Wight. (Six miles to orchestra practice in Newport instead of 20 to Hereford.)

My first visit to the Isle of Wight must have been about 1947, a day trip with my father on a paddle steamer from Portsmouth, to see my grandmother who was staying with friends in Seaview; I suppose we went from Ryde to Seaview on Seaview Services. While the elders nattered I was left to consume some spam … and ate the lot, with dire consequence. Notwithstanding the Isle of Wight, Seaview again, was a holiday destination, while my parents researched a guidebook to be published, with some success, by Batsford. The island remained a day-trip

BELOW: *Delight of Jowitt's late teenage years, was to trail through London suburbia on the diminishing tentacles of the (arguably) greatest trolleybus system in the world, this particular tentacle being the 647, Stamford Hill to London Docks. The trolleybus shown is typical of the immediate pre-war fleet.*

destination, both for dying railways and for further guide-books entrusted to my parents, the latter (books!) now being illustrated by my photographs, hurrah! From Herefordshire, however, the Island became a regular summer holiday, with Winchester friends who were the happy owners of a holiday cottage. It appeared at the time that residence on the Holiday Isle would prove a permanent holiday. Hmmm!

One bonus was I became inspanned into Southern Vectis events as a part-time driver, and took my turn on specials for the Isle of Wight Festivals and the like, involving a variety of buses which I would have considered modern save that with the increasing speed of the flight of years and the frequently less than perfect condition of such buses they were manifestly approaching the status of heroes of antiquity.

The other boon was proximity to Portsmouth, ferry port to Caen or Cherbourg or St Malo. You take a bus, a 1938 Underground train, a catamaran ferry and another bus and there you are aboard one of those splendid Brittany Ferries for a dashed good French meal and decent bunk (if you book in time, otherwise you risk the most uncomfortable night of your life, or nearly) and in the dawn all France and its still magical buses are before you. My tales of such explorations are to be found in earlier editions of this work, and indeed if you work back far enough you will find other of my adventures.

I can add that our Island is not ill placed for other devices, inasmuch as you repeat the performance above to Portsmouth Harbour and then a train to

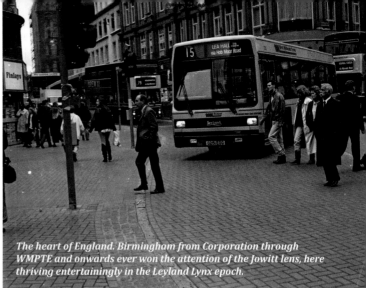

*The heart of England. Birmingham from Corporation through WMPTE and onwards ever won the attention of the Jowitt lens, here thriving entertainingly in the Leyland Lynx epoch.*

*In Lisbon the thoroughly British – except for being complete mirror-image - AEC Regent, still handsome if battered in 1976, had almost as much allure as the trams themselves, this sample revealing a youthful passenger alighting in classic style.*

Waterloo (quite often fairly reliable) and a 59 (now a Boris bus) to St Pancras for a Eurostar. Brought up in the era of proper cross-Channel boats I naturally deplore this fashion, you might as well be riding on the London Underground (except no stations) with complete lack of romance; but must admit it is convenient for points north and south from Brussels.

It so happened that in the first decade of the new millennium I had twofold cause to avail myself of this performance. My sister's bridesmaid (of 1970) had been busy typing my dear late mother's autobiographical notes but while my sister received a copy of the result I, despite repeated requests failed so to do, thus finally I said I would visit bridesmaid to collect a copy, to which bridesmaid readily agreed; it so happened she lived in Luxembourg.

The other cause for travel was that when I was photographing the marvellous muddle of mixed gauges of trams in Liege in 1959 I had encountered a young Dutchman engaged apparently upon the same pursuit. On my having addressed him, in English to his amazement, as to his purpose we exchanged addresses and promised to send to each other the results of our efforts and indeed other tramway matters, and verily continued in this vein the next half-century, and, following various intermediate meetings, resolved to meet for the fiftieth anniversary, which, with Liege devoid of the glory we had known, we settled upon his home of Rotterdam and rode round on one of the magnificent preserved central entrance bogie cars I had known 50 years before. To add to this, once or twice with one or another of my sons, I rendered several repeat visits. Thus I rejoiced in trams which had represented

*Forty or so years ago the Lisbon trams were almost still a close resemblance of any respectable tram system of the 1920s-1930s. At the Largo do Rato in 1976 (where there were choice wine taverns in the offing) we find typical cars, un-dateable because of many re-numberings or re-buildings but close to 1920s types or Portuguese semi-streamlined late 1940s.*

dreadful modernity when first encountered in the 1960s now proving entrancing antiquities, PCCs in Antwerp and so on, while dashes to Stuttgart and St Gallen produced articulated buses on four axles – such format as I had not seen since my youth in Germany, while Zurich offered three-part trolleybuses, along with trams not too different, some of them, from those I loved in days of yore. As for Luxembourg, every time I passed through, it offered a ceaseless tide of buses, I do not think I have ever seen so constant and regular an omnibus torrent. Be it noted this included three-part articulateds!

Let it be stated, however, lest I be deemed too European in my predilections, that if Birmingham or Bristol now proved beyond my orbit I had occasion to sample very intensive operation in Cambridge – because my daughter now lived there – and, *en passant*, in London. Here, though I deplored their presence as far too alien compared with the RTs and RMs which I considered proper to the issue, I had to admit to being much attracted to Red Ken's articulations and then, with their prompt ousting, by their Boris usurpers. Surely very splendid vehicles! Moreover I frequently travelled on Southern Vectis –

RIGHT: *Trams of which the ingress was dreaded by Jowitt in the 1960s as destroying the period joys he had loved were to prove, half a century later, charming survivals. This PCC car in Ghent, Belgium, while much modified and revamped over four or five decades, proves a fine example as it attacks a glorious piece of recently laid but classic style of point-work in 2017*

free, one of the few benefits of old age – and, passing by, noted various spots which I ought really to be using in very artistic compositions, shapely trees or sea-pinks on dramatic cliffs. I have in one or two instances actually achieved this aim.

Throughout these six decades I ever believed

ABOVE: *The main arteries of Luxembourg (while awaiting, in 2017, a new tramway) boast a peak service equal to or even more intensive than the golden age of London's Oxford Street. In the suburbs it is obviously less dense, and this café in the peaceful suburb of Bonnevoie is enjoying a quiet moment. But just wait until evening when the locals – mostly Portuguese – will emerge and the tables will be full! The bus, a Mercedes-Benz Citaro, shows a recent Luxembourg livery.*

that I did not especially like buses (compared with trolleybuses and above all trams) and most particularly I disliked modern buses such as Lodekkas, Leyland Nationals and Saviem SC10 standards. I came in due time to warm towards the latter – though Lodekkas and Nationals never won my heart – and as the years have fled I find I have rather better appreciated the newer offerings; perforce, perhaps, because with increasing draconian rules there is very little that might be described as verging on elderly to be encountered.

Some modernity these days could really be described as luxurious, yes, even normal service buses, upper decks such as you can encounter in Reading and Oxford and Blue Star on Southampton to Winchester route 1 with tables and sofas, are a very far cry from four wood-slat seats in a row with access from a trough a foot below deck-level.

I must admit to less than delight with modern tickets, though I have little to do with them, because as I have said I enjoy the freedom of potential senility, except on the continent where every outfit employs some different system, usually dispensed from gadgets on the pavement which despite being not unusually in four languages, some of which I speak fairly fluently, I find myself quite flummoxed

by the rules and instructions. I was brought up in the days of classic Edmondson-size Bell Punch, many colours overprinted with large price figures in other colours, and often with wonderful lists of names of fare stages. Contemporary Insert Setright – Edmondson size again - were far less attractive though returns with herring-bone control strip at either end boasted a certain charm. Up north there were curious tickets where the conductor chopped out a piece to the correct value, lovely big long wide tickets, or those curious specimens where the conductor had to write in pencil the fare on the ticket (with carbon underneath) and wind it out.

Progress came with the Ultimate, five or six rolls side by side, tickets half Edmondson size, thus only half the attraction. I knew them well in Bournemouth and on King Alfred. Then Setright and Gibson swept the whole scene clean and boring, though years and years later I came to appreciate what utterly splendid pieces of machinery these breeds are. I was very lucky that in my times on Vectis festival specials there was a bold revival of Setright employment in vogue, because I was far too Luddite ever to have overcome the complications of such affairs as Wayfarer.

I do not wish to harp overmuch on my antiquity, but I find increasingly the frailties of Old Age catching up with me, I am aware I could not tramp a whole day round a tram system as was my wont in days of yore. Moreover photography in the street is these days perhaps a risky operation, when what was once innocent study of passers by (admittedly including young ladies but also every sort of humanity and every degree of architecture besides) is now liable through hysteria and witch-hunting to be regarded as stalking or terrorist plotting.

Over the years I worked through from my mother's pre-war folding 620 to Ilford Sportsman to Braun Paxette to 2 ¼ sq Rolleicord to Bronica and sundry Zenith et al. I had worked almost exclusively in black-and-white until the new millennium whereafter I went for colour prints via cheap postal firms, less hard work and no nasty darkroom smells. Will it surprise you if I state that I never engaged in the world of digital? I am now not sure which will come first, the day when normal film processing is abandoned by any firm save obscure specialists on the internet, or the day when I decide to hang up for ever such as remain to me of that faithful fleet of cameras.

I am on the other hand quite sure that I will make no attempt to return for the anniversary to Paderborn... ∎

*A Red Ken artic in the heart of the Empire of Capitalism.*

BELOW: *West of Birmingham in the early 1990s was a hotbed of second-hand Leyland Nationals, with for Jowitt more charm than ever he had found in their youth and questionable beauty! The two in the foreground had been new to Crosville and Ribble.*

*After the artics came the Borismaster, here with a suitably modernistic background near Victoria.*

# VIEWED FROM A DIFFERENT ANGLE

**Tony Wilson** offers an alternative approach to bus photography.

ABOVE: *Tower Transit uses a fleet of eight Wright Pulsar-bodied VDL SB200 single-deckers on London service RV1, a kind of semi-tourist route from Covent Garden via Waterloo and the South Bank to Tower Hill. Having crossed over Waterloo Bridge, buses loop around by the London Eye and along Belvedere Road where 62996 pulls away from a bus stop bound for Tower Hill in August 2015. Taken from a bridge, this offers an excellent view of the hydrogen tanks and paraphernalia on the roof of the bus.*

How often do bus and coach pictures illustrate the vehicle's front or nearside three quarters aspects, generally on the horizontal, more often than not stationary at a bus stop, on a bus stand or parked up unattended? For many trade publications this is what is wanted, as vehicles are set up and photographs taken in order to show off their features to prospective customers. However, this really is not the case, as buses and coaches spend much of their time out and about operating through all kinds of terrain and negotiating hazards during their working days. Thus as the title suggests, what follows is a selection of buses and coaches going about their duties, but observed from different angles. ∎

ABOVE: *June 2005 in Barnsley and a few months before the Yorkshire Traction group was taken over by Stagecoach. Two Northern Counties Palatine I-bodied Volvo Olympians, 608/9, were at the bus and train Interchange. Originally these were owned by London Central.*

*The TransPeak route runs across the Peak District from Derby via Matlock, Bakewell, and Buxton to Manchester. Currently operated by the High Peak Bus Company out of Dove Holes, buses appear in this rather pleasant two-tone green livery. On the A5270 between the A6 and A515 roads the route ascends a rise that affords vistas across the verdant surroundings, and this is where in October 2012 near Chelmorton an opportunity arose to capture 788 (YN06 CJE), a Scania CN94UB OmniCity. However, what one cannot see and appreciate is the photographer atop a small step-ladder in order to gain more height.*

RIGHT: *With continued threats to bus services, especially the more rural routes, here is a nice little Dennis Mini Pointer Dart, FX54 LLE, from the Hornsbys of Scunthorpe fleet. Route 68 serves outlying villages on the Lincolnshire Wolds and one wonders how they are faring in current conditions. The location is Knabbs Bridge near Barnetby in North Lincolnshire in April 2015, which takes the roadway over the railway line between Grimsby and Cleethorpes.*

BELOW: *During July 1978 inclement weather and high winds led to sand from the beach at Poldhu Cove being deposited onto the road that curves its way along this part of the Cornish coastline on the Lizard Peninsula. Western National route 537 also wound its way through much of this territory as buses like Eastern Coachworks-bodied Bristol LH 1622 (KTT 37P) negotiated their way from the Lizard Point back to Helston.*

BELOW: *The walls of the old British Airways building in London's Victoria were oft frequented to provide a little bit of elevation, as buses and coaches passed through the junction of Buckingham Palace Road and Elizabeth Street on their way to or from Victoria Coach Station. Here with the Wessex subsidiary of the National Bus Company is ECW-bodied Leyland Olympian 50 (ADD 50Y), which was the forerunner of a small batch that were used as commuter coaches for companies which served London from the Home Counties. Operators that used them were Alder Valley, Eastern National, London Country Bus Services and Maidstone & District.*

*Bridges, both vehicular and pedestrian, provide good vantage points over the network of motorways to view the passing traffic. On an early evening during May 1985, at one such bridge over the M1 motorway near Edgware in Middlesex, rugby-supporting passengers filled East Yorkshire Motor Services' Eastern Coachworks-bodied Leyland Olympian 534 (B534 WAT) and several coaches as they return to their northern homes after a cup final match held at Wembley Stadium. The driver of the Smiths Happiways-Spencers Volvo isn't breaking the law; at this time coaches were permitted to use the outside lane of three-lane motorways.*

RIGHT: *The Jurassic coastline of Dorset has its ups and downs where magnificent views are afforded travellers as they venture along this interesting area of outstanding natural beauty. In June 2003, with the Chesil Beach and the Isle of Portland in the far distance, First Hampshire & Dorset 62408 (YS03 ZKE), a Wright Solar-bodied Scania L94UB makes easy work of the long ascent up from Abbotsbury, bound for Exeter.*

LEFT: *The Bridge of Sighs within the confines of Chester's ancient walls is a good vantage point to observe vehicles as they enter the city centre. Bound for one of the bus stations in April 2002, Chester City Transport 10 (F210 JMB), is a Northern Counties Palatine I-bodied Leyland Olympian. It had been repainted into a green base livery with cream and maroon stripes to celebrate 100 years of passenger transport service in the city.*

BELOW: *Stand on Waverley Bridge outside Edinburgh's main railway station and one can look up towards the main city centre thoroughfare of Princes Street. This all-Leyland Olympian demonstrator, G21 HHG, was on loan to Lothian Regional Transport in 1989 when it was observed from a lower angle as it turned down on to the bridge.*

ABOVE: *The wall of an adjoining road makes it easy to photograph buses of all sorts as they enter the bus station in Durham. February 2018 and one of Go North East's fleet of Optare Solo SR models, 654 (NK15 GDF) in pink Indigo network livery, proves the point.*

RIGHT: *West Yorkshire Road Car's ECW-bodied Bristol RE 1397 (NWU 322M) sits on layover beside the railway war memorial in York on Station Road. Once again it is the battlements of the city's walls that provide the elevated position, this time in September 1979. The bus looks relatively clean and perhaps refreshed from a recent repaint.*

ABOVE: *Was the Wright StreetCar a success? I leave others to debate the pros and cons of the design. It certainly turned a few heads when it first appeared, and a number of StreetCars were allocated by FirstBus to York. From the ancient walls of the city 19007 (YK06 ATY) curves its way from Station Road into Queen Street in August 2007, as it operates on cross-city route 4. Behind the bus there stand former railway structures alongside the current railway station on the East Coast Main Line.*

*Stagecoach operates route 78 from Keswick through Borrowdale to Seatoller at the eastern base of the Honister Pass. During the summer season this is run with open-toppers such as 17217 (V217 MEV). The origins of the bus, an Alexander ALX400-bodied Dennis Trident, lay in far different surroundings, as from 2000 it had pounded the streets of East London in closed top form on Transport for London's route network.*

BELOW: *During the early to mid 1970s Leicester City Transport acquired a fair fleet of Scanias with Metro-Cammell bodies in both double- and single-deck form. 136-153 and 209-225 were the single-deck versions from 1971 and some were still around in May 1984 including 209 (ARY 209K), seen from a walkway over St Nicholas Circle. Fuel prices at the Elf petrol station are 39.5p per litre or £1.79p per gallon.*